ROOTED IN THE HOOD

ORO
EDITIONS

Publishers of Architecture, Art, and Design
Gordon Goff: Publisher

www.oroeditions.com
info@oroeditions.com

Published by ORO Editions

Graphic Design & Text: Anna Angelidakis
Copy Editing: Cullen Thomas
Photo Retouching: TJ Gemignani
Map Illustrations: Donald Murphy
ORO Project Coordinator: Kirby Anderson

10 9 8 7 6 5 4 3 2 1 First Edition

Library of Congress data available upon request. World Rights: Available

ISBN: 978-1-943532-76-6

Color Separations and Printing: ORO Group Ltd.
Printed in China.

International Distribution: www.oroeditions.com/distribution

ORO Editions makes a continuous effort to minimize the overall carbon footprint of its publications. As part of this goal, ORO Editions, in association with Global ReLeaf, arranges to plant trees to replace those used in the manufacturing of the paper produced for its books. Global ReLeaf is an international campaign run by American Forests, one of the world's oldest nonprofit conservation organizations. Global ReLeaf is American Forests' education and action program that helps individuals, organizations, agencies, and corporations improve the local and global environment by planting and caring for trees.

ROOTED IN THE HOOD

AN INTIMATE PORTRAIT OF NEW YORK CITY'S COMMUNITY GARDENS

ANNA ANGELIDAKIS

CONTENTS

INTRODUCTION

Rooted in the Hood is a celebration of the community gardens of New York City and the people who create, cultivate, and enjoy them. The late '60s and '70s witnessed the devastation of New York with many buildings in low-income areas left unattended, burned, and reduced to rubble. Drug dealers, gangs and junkies soon moved in, making those neighborhoods unsafe to live.

This is a book about the ordinary people, dreamers, artists, and activists who rose up against these unsafe conditions, cleared empty lots, planted trees and vegetables, and slowly created small oases of peace and nature for the community.

According to GreenThumb, the largest community gardening program in the nation and part of the New York City Parks Department, there are at least five hundred and fifty gardens throughout the five boroughs, accounting for more than one hundred acres of open space.

From the orderly British countryside style of the Parque de Tranquilidad in Alphabet City, to the vegetable lots of Carver Community Garden in East Harlem, it's almost impossible to describe the many worlds and cultures.

INTRODUCTION

Joy, hope, spirituality, and a love of the absurd can be seen all around. A headless statue rests gently against a withered bridal wreath; a child's dinner set positioned under the powerful mural of a blue jay; an archangel holding a broken sword stands defeated below a blooming cherry tree.

The displays of art, flowers, and vegetation constantly change, drawing visitors back again and again, each return as fresh, and the experience as exhilarating as the first time. These places are rooted but mutable: royal-pink asters and sky-blue hydrangeas in summer; golden calendulas and burnt-sienna mums in autumn; bone-white snowdrops and boxwood in winter; an eruption of hues and fragrances each spring, as coral peonies and sweet-scented lilacs bloom everywhere.

In 2008 my father, a sea captain in the Greek Merchant Marine, passed away. I found myself looking for quiet places to gather my thoughts. On one of these walks I noticed a gate at the corner of 9th Street and Avenue C with the welcoming sign, "The garden is open."

I entered unaware of how this small step was to change my life. Maybe it was the tall, willow-tree foliage swaying in the wind, or the startling blue eyes of a ceramic geisha, but I knew I had found a home, and it wasn't just this garden I discovered. I started to *see* what had always been before me, but I'd never noticed, small enclaves of greenery each one more pristine and enchanting than the one before it.

The more I read about the history of New York City's community gardens, and their struggle to reclaim the devastated lots of the '70s and '80s, the more fascinated I became. A world had opened before me, and it was impossible to go back and close the gate.

Since 2009, I've walked through the gardens photographing them through all seasons. My small camera not only freed my movements, but allowed people to relax and let me take their photographs.

My goal was to learn and discover. I wanted to remain as discreet as possible, and let the people and gardens narrate the story.

INTRODUCTION

Originally, my attention was focused in my neighborhood, the Lower East Side, but soon I expanded my search to the West Side and Harlem, both East and West. As for the other four boroughs, Queens, Brooklyn, the Bronx, and Staten Island, they're under exploration.

Some gardens allowed me to photograph them with ease. The light was perfect and the composition strong. Others proved a great challenge. Some gardens slowly relented, others remained defiant til the end. Nothing was ever static. As in a gallery, nature made sure to alter the display with different colors and hues. Objects disappeared only to reappear in a different location or a nearby garden. New items magically emerged.

Photograph by photograph, I came to know the most intimate corners of each garden. I met ordinary people with extraordinary lives, people whose struggles put my own life into perspective, some born in other countries, just like me, and for whom these small plots were both an anchor in this new world and a reference to their ancestral land.

My initial shyness and hesitance to talk to strangers were quickly replaced by trust. Some residents took pride in growing fruit trees and vegetables, others in growing beautiful flowers. Some gardens were meticulously kept and others left almost unattended, poignantly revealing socioeconomic differences and the varied character of the city.

These gardens remain vital parts of their neighborhoods, with live performances, song and dance, poetry readings, workshops on sustenance and gardening, and a celebration of the seasons. Weddings, birthdays, graduations, and memorials are often conducted in the shade of their trees, the entire community invited.

The idea of combining this history and these experiences into a book came gradually, like a seed slowing taking root. Once the idea was born, everything else fell magically together; connections occurred, and similar minded people came together. The New York City I thought I knew, reinvented itself, and I rediscovered her, from the ground up, in the most profound way. So, this photo essay is a book of love and thanks.

LOWER EAST SIDE COMMUNITY GARDENS

1. Liz Christy Garden
2. Elizabeth Street Garden
3. M'Finda Kalunga Garden
4. Le Petit Versailles Garden
5. All People's Garden, Inc.
6. Kenkeleba House Garden
7. Los Amigos
8. Parque De Tranquilidad
9. El Jardin Del Paraiso
10. 6BC Botanical Garden
11. 6th Street & Avenue B Garden
12. Green Oasis Community Garden/ Gilbert's Garden
13. Earth People
14. 9th Street Community Garden & Park
15. La Plaza Cultural-Armando Perez Community Garden
16. Campos Community Garden
17. El Sol Brillante Garden
18. Dias Y Flores

Houston

In 1973, artist Liz Christy and her band of volunteers transformed a vacant lot at this site to create the Bowery-Houston Community Farm and Garden. Her Green Guerillas cleared garbage, built soil from police-stable manure, and planted trees, flowers, and vegetables.

More than 600 community gardens now grace New York City neighborhoods.

Generations of volunteer gardeners have enhanced the design, recruited members, and opened this garden to the public weekends and some evenings.

In 2004, the garden faced an existential threat from the development of surrounding lots by AvalonBay. Thanks to action from garden members, the community, city officials and the Parks Department, the garden not only survived but was expanded to Second Avenue.

The Liz Christy Garden is famous worldwide for its beauty as well as its unlikely formation. With its dedicated, all-volunteer membership, it continues to prosper even as the neighborhood changes.

Garden volunteers at beginnings, Spring 1974
Top left: Dawn redwood, Metasequoia glyptostroboides, planted in 1975
Top right: In 2005, demolition of Church of All Nations came within inches of the garden

FIRST NEW YORK CITY COMMUNITY GARDEN

LIZ CHRISTY GARDEN

Namesaver of Liz Christy Garden during its early period

WINDOWS ON THE BOWERY

The Bowery is NYC's oldest thoroughfare. Originally a Native American footpath and Dutch farm road (bouwerij means farm), it is a cradle of American culture, with seminal links to tap dance, vaudeville, Yiddish theater, Lincoln, Stephen Foster, Irving Berlin, tattoo art, Abstract Expressionism, Beat literature, jazz and punk rock. Though listed on the National Register of Historic Places, out of scale developments are displacing its residents, small businesses, and historic character. More info, link to Bowery's National Register listing: boweryalliance.org

Funding for the BOWERY SIGNAGE PROJECT: Liz Abzeg Fund, Puffin Foundation, Partisan...
Andre Balazs, Adam Woodward, John Dohan, Michael A. Lewis Architect, and contributions from Bowery friends and neighbors. Poster design: Professional Practice Clinic, The Cooper Union.

BOWERY ALLIANCE OF NEIGHBORS

1

LIZ CHRISTY COMMUNITY GARDEN

Liz Christy. No book on community gardens could ever be complete without mentioning her many contributions to the community gardens movement.

A local resident, graphic designer, and painter, Liz teamed up with a group of gardening activists to form the Green Guerillas. These activists planted vacant lots with window boxes, tree pits, and "seed bombs," setting down the roots for the many varieties of trees and green neighborhood spaces that we enjoy today.

The "seed bombs" were balloons stuffed with peat moss, fertilizer, and wildflower seeds, which Liz and the green guerillas threw into fenced-off lots around the five boroughs, an act of civil disobedience against a city administration that refused to take ownership of the dire conditions in many neighborhoods.

WEBSITE:
lizchristygarden.us

ADDRESS
E. Houston Street, between Second Avenue & Bowery

HOURS
All year:
Sat: Noon – 4 p.m.
Sun: Noon – 4 p.m.
May – Sept:
Tue & Th: 6 p.m. – Dusk

Entrance sign with brief history, featuring Liz Christy in the original garden

As the story goes, during a very cold winter, four homeless people were found frozen in the lot under their cardboard boxes, which horrified the community. Shorty afterwards, as Liz was walking in the Bowery she saw a group of children playing around an old refrigerator, in the same lot, unaware of the danger. This solidified the group's commitment to take action.

Driving in Liz's beat-up Datsun, the Green Guerillas scattered their seed bombs, giving birth to the community gardens of Manhattan.

Luscious apricots ready to be picked

The Liz Christy Garden opened in 1973 and is considered the oldest community garden in the city. There is a reverence about this place as if Liz's spirit is immortalized in every tree and rock. Walking the grounds today, amidst the flowers and the indigenous plants, you can hardly imagine the many difficult conditions those young green pioneers and gardeners had to face.

However, they prevailed, like the plants and flowers each year. They built a legacy of something natural and pure in this wild city.

Window overlooking the garden at dusk

2

ELIZABETH STREET GARDEN

Elizabeth Street Gallery owner Allan Reiver leased this lot in the early '90s, and fulfilled his promise to the neighborhood by cleaning it up, landscaping the grounds, and filling it with statues from his gallery, creating an outdoor museum.

Allan planted pear trees, installed a gravel path, and built a barn that is used for public events, exhibits, and gatherings. Over the years, the garden has blossomed and flourished.

Today the place is brimming with life, as people bask under the sunlight amidst lion and sphinx statues or stretch on blankets under the gentle eyes of the goddess Hebe and a young Bacchus.

There is artistry and care in these grounds, attracting locals and visitors alike. Nothing is left to chance. Each path leads to a discovery, a hidden treasure, giving the impression that one has entered upon magical grounds.

Iconic lion statue entangled with vine; circa 1850-1890.

WEBSITE:
elizabethstreetgarden.com

ADDRESS
Elizabeth Street

HOURS
Spring:
Week Days: Noon – 5 p.m.
Weekends: 10 a.m. – 5 p.m.
Summer:
Week Days: Noon – 6 p.m.
Weekends: 10 a.m. – 6 p.m.
Fall:
Week Days: Noon – 5 p.m.
Weekends: 10 a.m. – 5 p.m.
Winter:
Week Days: Noon – 4 p.m.
Weekends: Noon – 4 p.m.

Recently the Elizabeth Street Garden has become the center of a classic battle between those pushing for housing and development, and environmentalists, green-space advocates, and other quality-of-life residents. Green space is precious, a fine cause. Affordable housing for low-income seniors is also a good cause. Both sides raise legitimate questions, but green spaces are disappearing faster and faster.

The garden, open from dawn to dusk, is embedded with the spirit and history of the community; it's home to old and young alike.

Left: Guardian Sphinx; Right: 1. Medusa Head 2. Hebe, Goddess of Youth 3. Copper boy removing nail 4. Watchful dog

It's hard to imagine the neighborhood without the many activities offered in the garden, from the Halloween costume making and parade, to the fall harvest and the celebration of the winter solstice, to summer concerts and theater performances.

The new housing development was approved by the city council in 2019. It remains unclear how much of the beloved garden, visited and enjoyed by tens of thousands of New Yorkers every year, will be preserved. Let's hope a compromise can be reached.

Left: Young Bacchus; Right: Harvest Goddess

3

M'FINDA KALUNGA GARDEN

In the African language of Kikongo, the M'Finda Kalunga garden is the "Garden at the Other Side of the World," a sacred space where the dead live in harmony and plenitude.

New York City's second African burial ground, this powerful place has a rich history, as well as a strong contemporary presence.

The garden hosts many cultural festivals, such as Halloween/Samhain, Chinese Moon Festival, Juneteenth, Cinco de Mayo, and Sukkot. It also offers gardening programs, readings, movie nights, planting days, and a Bocce tournament, a game from Roman times, brought to New York by Italian immigrants.

Tables and benches dot the winding paths, creating moments of reprieve, while a children's sandbox, a chicken coop, and a pond with turtles and golden orange koi attract young and old.

WEBSITE:
mkgarden.org

ADDRESS
165 Forsyth Street

HOURS
Summer, Spring and Fall:
Thu: 5 p.m. – 7 p.m.
Sat: 10 a.m – 4 p.m.
Sun: 12 p.m. – 4 p.m.

Figure from the series "Standing Strong: A Children's Garden of Mosaic Art," created in 2005 by neighborhood children in response to the September 11th attacks

A series of mosaic figures surround the perimeter of the garden, guardians of the inside and the outside world. The figures were created in response to the September 11th attacks and its impact on children.

In 2005 under the supervision of ECHO Prosocial Gallery, thirty children between the ages of seven and seventeen were selected to take part in the project. These young artists traced their silhouettes and decorated them with glass tiles and weather-resistant materials. The work is called *Standing Strong: A Children's Garden of Mosaic Art*.

Left: Volunteer at the garden entrance chatting with local man; Right: 1. Mosaic figure with American flags 2. Blooming roses 3. Turtle basking in the sun 4. Mosaic woman lost in foliage

4

LE PETIT VERSAILLES GARDEN

Spring has arrived and Le Petite Versailles's gates are open like the swallows returning from the South. The smell of winter still lingers, as piles of leaves wait to be cleared by Peter Cramer and Jack Waters, the founders and essence of this garden.

Le Petite Versailles is a project of Allied Productions, a non-profit organization that supports theater, film making, and the arts. Years of hard labor and love have established this small space as one of the most important artistic venues in the city.

The garden can be eerily quiet or filled with energy as artists move around setting up props and microphones for an evening's performance. Narrow beds filled with shrubs, perennials, vines, and annuals often function as extensions of the art displays adding another level of creativity.

WEBSITE:
alliedproductions.org/le-petit-versailles

ADDRESS
247 E. 2nd Street

HOURS
Thu – Sun: 2 p.m. – 7 p.m. or when the gate is open

Lord Shiva amidst offerings, overlooking the garden

The garden has two entrances, making the setting even more elusive. Stepping inside is like stepping into another dimension, never knowing what you'll encounter at the other side.

A stage dominates the garden's center. Performances take place under dimly lit candles, as exotic music fills the neighborhood. Lord Shiva, in the form of the cosmic, ecstatic dancer, with crystals and offerings at his feet, watches over this creative garden. French palace, Hindu god, men and women, the nature of this city.

Left: Iconic sign; Right: 1. Broken mirrors reflecting the light 2. Remaining garlands from an old performance 3. Colorful banner 4. Center stage

Macarena Summers

Glamour

5

ALL PEOPLE'S GARDEN

Late autumn, leaves swirl and chase each other on the empty pavements. Tucked near the end of 3rd street and Avenue D, the garden feels abandoned, almost desolate, but the gate is open and the sun is bursting through the clouds, so I enter.

The rays land on the murals of two women, Olean Cowart For, visionary and founder of the garden, and Macarena Summers, a local resident. The murals are bold, conveying strength, but also kindness and playfulness. This humbles me. These unselfish volunteers have so much to teach me about community service and endurance.

I walk around tenderly, as if not to disturb the dormant spirits. The silence is hypnotic, almost alluring. The melancholy of the place matches my own, it makes me think of the passage of time, beginnings and endings, the true life of a garden.

WEBSITE:
grownyc.org/openspace/
gardens/man/all-peoples

ADDRESS
293 E. 3rd Street
between Avenues C & D

HOURS
Seasonal or when the gate
is open

Mural of Macarena Summers Glamour, 2010

On another day, now winter, it's snowing and the wind is blistering cold. The garden looks more foreboding than ever and the colors of the murals have lost their luster. A homeless man has found shelter inside the gazebo. Without the garden and this small space of solace, this man may have frozen from the cold.

Summer now for All People. The garden feels exuberant, filled with light and life. Gone are the feelings of isolation and dread. Flowers bloom everywhere, in complete contrast with the previous months.

Left: Blooming stargazer; Right: 1. Young girl with smoothie 2. Gazebo 3. Mural of Olean Cowart For, founder 4. Woman in summer hat

The place overflows with community spirit. The paths are swept and the winter debris collected. The murals shine, reinvigorated by golden sunlight. People are gathered around the stage. There's fresh lemonade and homemade pound cake. Children run around chasing each other and taking turns on the rocking horse. A woman, in festive clothing and a large brim hat, starts playing the flute and another, with a powerful voice, sings gospels. Her voice rises above the fence, filling the neighborhood. People clap, and the old, young, and homeless, unite.

Left: Summer light illuminating the performance stage; Right: The garden under a thick coat of snow

6

KENKELEBA HOUSE GARDEN

Mysterious. What kind of spirits inhabit this garden, named for a West African plant, earthbound and yet free as the clouds? Pain and struggle, power and gentleness. What messages do they transmit, or is it their silence that says it all?

Kenkeleba House Garden is exclusively dedicated to African American artists and other artists of color. Frequently ignored by the mainstream establishment and galleries, these artists and their works are powerfully rooted in this space, a proof that art and creativity are the inherit right of all.

A man, his head titled sideways, looks at the sky. Is it defiance or suffering? Day after day, arms folded, unprotected from the rain and the wind. Always alone. That other sculpture, intriguing and whimsical, an alien creature made out of steel and stained glass.

WEBSITE:
kenkeleba.org

ADDRESS
214 E. 2nd Street
between Avenues B & C

HOURS
When the gate is open or by appointment at kenkeleba@msn.com

Left: Uzikee Nelson, "Bobo. The Flying Man," 1992 (steel, stained glass)
Right: Helen Evans Ramsaran, "Sanctuary Group," 1993 (bronze with white patina)

The fence between us creates a boundary that I cannot cross, yet
I crave to understand what keeps them so ethereal and yet so earth bound.

An old motorcycle, rusty now—whose powerful frame did it once carry?
Whose lungs breathed the air believing that all was possible?

A rusted battleship. My father created a similar one on one of his
sea travels. Did the sculptor and my father share similar experiences?
There's a message in this garden, each figure standing isolated, while
outside the fence, I keep trying to find an entrance to their world.

Left: 1. Linus Coraggio, "Scrap Metal World," 2014 (welded steel, cast iron and forged iron) 2. Anonymous, "Untitled, Head," (anonymous installation) 3. Artis Lane, "Amistad," 1998 (bronze with black patina) 4. Natalie Giugni, "World Lair," 2011 (found materials)
Right: Linus Coraggio, "Tall, dapper Derby man who holds the key," 1994 (welded steel and cast iron)
Following page: Linus Coraggio, "Vietnam Chopper," 1994 (found materials)

7

LOS AMIGOS GARDEN

Angelina, the name of a tiny boat floating on turquoise-blue waters towards Castillo San Cristobal, another enchanting mural by the local artist Chico. The colors are bright, exuberant, as people with outstretched arms encounter their beloved city.

A second mural, with a yellow dove carrying an olive branch against a blue background with stars; a Puerto Rican flag swaying in the wind; a traditional casita decorated with old masks, all part of this magical world.

There's a lightness in this garden and a sense of well being. A man, his face open like the brightly-lit sky above, welcomes me and shows me the grapevine, the pride of the garden. I tell him I'm from Greece, and that we grow vines everywhere. "So beautiful," he answers. "I have a friend who went there."

WEBSITE:
Unavailable

ADDRESS
221 E. 3rd Street
between Avenues B & C

HOURS
Seasonal or when the gate
is open

Dove and white roses by muralist Antonio "Chico" Garcia

"Like Puerto Rico, filled with sunlight," I add, although I've never been there. The man's smile widens.

On another day in this garden, a woman greets me, broom in hand, chasing after leaves from last night's thunderstorm. She is meticulous, efficient. I remember the whitewashed walls and carefully tended gardens of Greece. This place speaks to my heart.

Winter. Los Amigos now is covered in thick snow, but never losing its magic, like a smile of mutual respect.

Left: "Castillo San Cristobal," by muralist Antonio "Chico" Garcia; Right: 1. Puerto Rican Day Parade 2. Aztec pyramid 3. Garden and mural after the first snow 4. Gardener under trellis

8

PARQUE DE TRANQUILIDAD

Never has a garden been more aptly named. Serenity finds you before you even enter, a heaven of color and scents tucked away in a small street of Alphabet City. Flowers everywhere, from the most striking hibiscus and hydrangeas to antique roses, tulips, and day lilies. Every season welcomed and recorded along these winding stone-dust paths, even winter, when the tiny snowcaps shyly pop out from the earth.

But it's Anne Boster and Jutta Neumann that make all the difference. Permanent fixtures of the garden, they're often seen with a basket of tools in one hand, and a water hose in the other, tending the grounds. They are the "human component" of the garden, welcoming people throughout the day, sometimes even opening the garden in the off hours, if one wishes to visit.

WEBSITE:
parquedetranquilidad.org

ADDRESS
314-318 E. 4th Street
between Avenues C & D

HOURS
Sun: 10 a.m. – 6 p.m. or when the gate is open

Blooming tulips and butterfly

Anne's gentle approach to planting marks her German-British heritage, while Jutta's artistry in handmade leather goods, attests to her creativity and preference for bold colors.

In one of my visits, Ann points with pride at a cluster of rusty foxglove: "This color is very rare, take as many pictures as you want."

When I arrive home I realize that all my shots are blurry, a sign that the flower did not want me to capture its beauty. Elusiveness retained. The magic still unnamed.

Left: English-inspired garden in bloom; Right: 1. Enchanting bluebells 2. Sunday coffee and cake 3. Gardener, Anne Boster 4. After the rain

When Ann is not pruning or planting, she feeds the neighborhood cats. A big gray male is her favorite. "Don't come too close," she advises, "he doesn't want anyone to touch him, including me." At the same time, the cat refuses to eat unless Ann places his bowl next to her.

Yula, at the other side of the garden, prepares for another Sunday coffee gathering with home-made biscuits and crumb cake.

If the garden was not named Tranquility then it could be called Garden of Grace, a true oasis and one close to my heart.

Left: Foxglove flowers; Right: Mother and child enjoying a summer stroll in the garden

9

EL JARDIN DEL PARAISO

A circular tree-house surrounding a willow tree, branches swirling upwards trying to catch a glimpse of sunlight. Children playing hide and seek; teenagers declaring their eternal love, writing on the tree's bench: "I love you. Be mine forever." Others, angry against the system, mixing curse words with wisdom: "You're not dead until someone shoots you."

El Jardin del Paraiso combines a man-made woodland, wetland, and meadow, not an easy task when there was once nothing but trash, old tires, and hypodermic needles in this plot.

The garden is mostly known for its medicinal plots where people of the community are free to harvest. Stinging nettle, motherwort, echinacea, feverfew, and goldenseal are a few of the varieties that grow on the grounds.

WEBSITE:
eljardindelparaiso.org

ADDRESS
710 E. 5th Street
between Avenues C & D

HOURS
Sat – Sun: 2 p.m. – 7 p.m.
or when the gate is open

Tree nest created by tree house architect and resident Roderick Romero

In the summer months, there are workshops on how to use plants and herbs for medicinal purposes, performances, cookouts and concerts that bring families together and strengthen the community.

For me, it's the man across the garden, always sitting on the brownstone steps listening to old blues, who best represents the spirit of this neighborhood. Observant, he always smiles and nods with recognition. Sometimes, others join him smoking cigarettes, hardly talking, always watching the rhythms of paradise.

Left: Pondering man in foliage; Right: Angel statue made out of clay in pink dress and blue wings

10

6BC BOTANICAL GARDEN

Turrets and chimneys interlaced with ivy; Rapunzel in her tower waiting for her beloved prince, her golden braid gently caressing the earth. Colors and flowers everywhere; swirling paths that lead to hidden corners; birds tweeting among the thick trellises.

A place so magical it draws you in like a fairytale, enchanting you to return again and again. Appropriately designated a botanical garden, the 6BC Botanical Garden is deeply devoted to bio-diversity, horticultural education, cultural activities and community programming.

The love and care in this garden are displayed everywhere, from the meticulously pruned trees and flowers, to the gentle pathways and awe-inspiring art installations and exhibits, all the way to the wooden house, also known as "The Library."

WEBSITE:
6bcgarden.org/

ADDRESS
630 E. 6th Street
between Avenues B & C

HOURS
April to October 31st
Sat – Sun: Noon – 6 p.m.
Mon – Fr: 6 p.m. – Dusk

"Whispers in the Grove," interactive, multimedia sculpture by Kathy Creutzburg, Natalia Lesniak and Mirabai Howard-Geoghan

The library is a dreamy place with majestic views of the grounds, filled with books and old photographs. It could be easily mistaken as a small cabin in the woods, somewhere deep in the forests of the Adirondacks or Maine. Everything about this room is endearing; the creaking floor; the weathered Middle Eastern rug; and the small balcony with the iron table and chairs.

The garden hosts many activities, concerts, art shows, and poetry readings. A place of nourishing and imagination.

Left: Brownstone overlooking the garden; Right: 1. Wooden house, also known as "The Library" 2. Welcoming signs 3. White peonies 4. Cascading wisteria; Following page: Winter wonderland

11

6TH STREET AND AVENUE B GARDEN

The "shy boy," that's what I called him when I first saw him hidden below the thick ivy. A small limestone statue with lowered eyes holding in his arm a newborn lamb. Who brought him here, condemning him to such obscurity, to see and hear all, but rarely to be seen unless one looks carefully? To endure the snow and the rain and record the garden's memories, asking for nothing? Or was the shy boy's obscuring simply nature taking over, in what once may have been an open plot?

In fact, in the '70s and early '80s, this corner was occupied by crumbling buildings used as "shooting galleries" by drug addicts. Then the city removed the buildings, and street association members and activists petitioned the city's Operation Green Thumb for permission to make the space a garden.

WEBSITE:
newsite.6bgarden.org

ADDRESS
630 E. 6th Street
between Avenues A & B

HOURS
April to October 31st
Sat – Sun: 1 p.m. – 6 p.m.
or when the gate is open

Meditating statue in green and terracotta tones

For a while the garden was in dispute, on the auction block, but in the end the activists, gardeners, planners, and artists won.

The garden of discovery and learning; that's what the 6 & B Garden is about. Hidden treasures to be unearthed and community stories to be shared under the summer stars. Gracious Buddha statues charmed with pink tulips; miniature Aztec warriors shooting arrows amidst the foliage. A water carrier, his green and orange robes long faded, guarding the small pond where koi glide by.

Left: Blooming tulips; Right: 1. Tin can rooster 2. Buddha statue in a bed of tulips 3. Autumn foliage 4. "Shy" boy with lamb

Today, the garden serves as a nexus for the neighborhood. Numerous workshops and classes are held here on planting, composting, recycling, and other abiding skills. Plant sales, pumpkin painting, costume contests, and Christmas decorating add another playful dimension in this garden.

As for the shy boy, he has been removed. Maybe he didn't survive the wind and the rain; nature can be brutal that way. Still, I keep coming back searching for him for a last glimpse, and to give him a heartfelt thank you for luring me into the garden.

Left: Peacock-inspired windmill; Right: Performance stage created by volunteers, with mural of New York rising out of exotic flowers

12

GREEN OASIS COMMUNITY GARDEN & GILBERT'S SCULPTURE GARDEN

Impressions: a Japanese garden where koi happily float; a bright red gazebo decorated with pink and red garlands; a charcoal board listing the members' tasks, smudged over by a child's flower drawing. A wooden table where people share food, watch performances, and celebrate the changes of seasons. Here is the spirit of Reynaldo Arenas, famous poet, theater aficionado, and one of the garden's founders.

Where the path seems to end, it begins again, meandering through colorfully painted boxes where bees gather pollen, leading to Gilbert's Garden, the sister garden of Green Oasis.

It was Ingram Gilbert, a local sculptor, along with Norman Valle, an ex-marine, and Reynaldo Arenas who decided to create a safe space for the neighborhood.

WEBSITE:
greenoasisnyc.org

ADDRESS
372 E. 8th Street
between Avenues C & D

HOURS
May to October 31st
Sat – Sun: 11 a.m. – 5 p.m.

Garden and red gazebo in snow

Today, Gilbert's wooden sculptures rise from the earth, organic, primeval, survivors of these hard times. Placed in a circle, the figures create a powerful display of African American art.

A woman rising from the earth with her hands raised upwards stands near a man whose head is encircled by a serpent. Another woman with strong African American features commands the circle; maybe she is Matilda, Gilbert's wife, to whom these sculptures are dedicated. Visible and invisible messages everywhere.

Sculptures created by self-taught Lower East Side artist Ingram Gilbert from materials found in the neighborhood

Yet the sculptures speak to everyone, proving the power of belonging to such a diverse community. A safe haven for all, it's not uncommon to encounter neighborhood cats roaming around the sculptures or basking in the sun. A raised shed, created by the garden's volunteers, keeps them warm and well-fed, with the added treat of a rodent. Connected: people, animals, and nature. An unbroken circle for all to take notice and safeguard.

Left: Last standing leaf; Right: Gilbert's garden with statues and cat

13

EARTH PEOPLE COMMUNITY GARDEN

How many pink flamingos can you count? Small and large ones, openly displayed or playfully hidden within the foliage. You might as well have landed in the Bahamas, or Aruba, except that you're still on the Lower East Side. Shimmering under the summer sun or huddling under the snow, the flamingos are always here, sentinels of the garden. If one falls, a new one replaces it. As long as the garden remains, so do the flamingos.

Stuffed animals, bears, monkeys, lions, and tigers hang from the trees or sit in half-broken chairs, withered from the wind and the rain, constantly watching.

"I love you," declares a faded red ribbon around a bear's waist, a Valentine past. A yawning lion, one eye missing, keeps guard at the entrance. Next to it a broken toy soldier speaks of happier days.

WEBSITE:
Unavailable

ADDRESS
333 E. 8th Street
between Avenues A & B

HOURS
May to October 31st
Sat – Sun: Noon – 5 p.m.

Welcoming flamingo at the garden gate

On the weekends a small flea market takes place in front of the garden, where neighborhood women display racks of clothes, shoes, electrical appliances, and chinaware. Other neighbors stop by rampaging through the piles, lifting hats and sandals, then tossing them away, complaining that they're too expensive or not well made. It's never the sales that matter, but the ritual of meeting to exchange news and gossip, a form of communal bonding that reminds me of the old women in Greek villages pulling out wooden chairs in the street, their laughter echoing deep into the night.

Left: Garden in winter; Right: 1. Flamingos in spring 2. Playful windmills 3. Flamingo and fabric flowers 4. Happy cow

14

9TH STREET COMMUNITY GARDEN AND PARK

The seasons are changing again: spring. The light turns sharper, focused, as details and colors emerge. A butterfly hovers above a pink rose bush, then flutters away. Irises, alliums, and chives stretch their stems towards the morning light, as golden carp glide gracefully in the pond's cool water. Everything is alive here, eager to affirm life.

I amble along the paths, drawing in the scent of the milk-white peonies and columbines. There's always a hidden treasure to be discovered; a salamander made out of crystal shards; a porcelain geisha, her violet eyes matching the blooming irises; a rusty weathervane horse entangled in a wisteria vine.

Sometimes I find feathers ceremoniously placed around rocks or clay amulets, all a part of this imaginative garden.

WEBSITE:
facebook.com/
9thstreetcommunitygardenpark

ADDRESS
703 E. 9th Street
corner of Avenue C

HOURS
April to October 31st
Fr: 5 p.m. – 8 p.m.
Sat – Sun: Noon – 6 p.m.
or when the gate is open

Garden detail, lizard with sparkling rhinestones

Maria, one of the gardeners, silently greets me, then disappears behind a rhododendron. Maria has pale eyes and always wears head-scarfs that accentuate her high cheekbones. She must be in her seventies, although her disposition makes her seem much younger.

When I praise the work done in the garden, she says, "it's nothing other than planting seeds; the rest is taken care of by nature." When I tell her how sad I feel about the willow trees brought down by the storm, Sandy, she shrugs. "Other things will grow," she answers.

Left: The garden in full bloom; Right: 1. Christmas day 2. Crimson roses 3. Cat tail flowers 4. Head of porcelain Geisha

The garden is a perfect example of the traditional "casitas," or "little houses," that were introduced in Alphabet City in the '50s and '60s when the first island-born Puerto Ricans arrived in the area. Located at the far end of the garden, the casita is an elevated wooden structure painted in lush colors. A Puerto Rican flag always marks its entrance, with a shrine dedicated to the Virgin Mary found nearby. Flowers, candles, and small tin offerings are displayed at her feet, homage to her compassion, and healing powers.

Left: The garden decked in snow; Right: Buddha amidst growing tulips, early spring

I'm about to walk away when I notice a boy, no more than five, trying to untangle a hose under his grandfather's watchful eyes. The water comes up abruptly, splashing his shoes.

"Be careful," the grandfather cautions him. "Water is precious and not to be wasted."

The boy laughs, his attention focused on an orange-yellow butterfly. He extends his hands towards her, butterfly and boy now waltzing around, disappearing behind the rose bushes.

Left: 1. Halloween scarecrow 2. Climbing roses 3. Water lilies 4. Maria Soares; Right: Plant illuminated by setting sun

15

LA PLAZA CULTURAL – DE ARMANDO PEREZ COMMUNITY GARDEN

When I think of La Plaza Cultural, all I see are colors. I see blue-green ribbons swaying back and forth; "Papa Bois," the father of the forest in the Trinidad tradition, an enormous paper mache mask, rising into the air, as "Mama Dlo," the mother of the river, follows behind, her limbs twisting into a serpent.

I see willow trees cascading over a fence festooned with detergent bottles, old tin cans, scrap metal, beer caps, and Rolando Politi's sculptures named, *Winter Flowers*.

Rolando, a spirited 70-year-old Italian-born anarchist and squatter is known as the trash worship artist of the Lower East Side. A permanent and beloved fixture of the neighborhood, Rolando's presence is visible everywhere within this garden.

WEBSITE:
laplazacultural.com

ADDRESS
674 E. 9th Street
between Avenues B & C

HOURS
April to October 31st
Sat – Sun: 10 a.m. – 7 p.m.
or when the gate is open

Rikki Asher, *"For the women of South Africa, Central America and the Lower East Side"* (1985); part of a larger mural titled *"La Lucha Continua, The Struggle Continues,"* 1985 & 2017

I see *La Lucha Continua, the Struggle Continues*, the remaining section of an enormous mural painted by international artists in the '70s. The mural, under the auspice of Eva Cockcroft, director of the Artmakers Inc., dealt with issues such as gentrification, police brutality, feminism and opposition to U.S. intervention to Central America.

It was in that same era, the late '70s, that the La Plaza Cultural garden was born. Local residents and greening activists rescued this vacant lot from garbage, drugs, and neglect.

Left: "Mama Dlo," the mother of the river in Trinidad tradition

The Latino group CHARAS, an acronym for its founders Chino, Humberto, Angelo, Roy, Anthony, and Sal, stepped in to help clean up. The group worked with the remarkable architect and visionary Buckminster Fuller, the Green Guerillas pioneer Liz Christy, and the artist Gordon Matta-Clark, who helped construct the amphitheater.

In 2002, La Plaza Cultural achieved legal preservation, and the year after was renamed in honor of Armando Perez, a CHARAS founder and community leader of the Lower East Side.

Right: Roses blooming with iconic neighborhood blue building in the background

In 2019 the fence, deemed unsafe by the city, had to be torn down. So were the willow trees, which succumbed to Hurricane Sandy's furry. Rolando's flowers are now scattered among nearby gardens, changing the feel of La Plaza Cultural de Armando Perez.

When I tell Rolando of how different everything looks, he shrugs. "Nothing is permanent," he declares. "The soil needed tending and the willows have a short life span. Maybe this time, we'll plant fruit trees, a wiser and far more useful choice."

Left: "Salvation Energy," by Zio Ziegler; Right: 1. Autumnal Sculpture 2. Crochet stitching figure 3. Farewell performance to the fallen willow trees by artist Theresa Byrnes 4. Archangel Michael; Following page: "Winter Flowers," by Rolando Politi, made out of found objects; the flowers have since been removed to restore the garden's fence

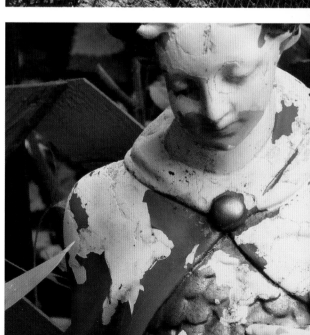

16

CAMPOS COMMUNITY GARDEN

Eagle feathers and seashells tangling in the wind, in a man's memory. The plot is shallow but his presence reaches deep, planting roots into the earth. I don't know who this man is, nor his history, but from his photograph and this tribute I can say he was loved and cared for, like the golden marigolds planted around him.

"Take whatever you need," a woman tells me, smiling from behind a vegetable bed.

This quiet place is part of the "green corridor," a cluster of gardens existing on East 12th Street. Everything that grows here is organic and the produce is shared with the entire neighborhood, bringing together an often forgotten community.

A mural painted by the local children, called *Save the Earth*, frames the entrance, addressing the environment.

WEBSITE:
camposcommunitygarden.org

ADDRESS
644 E. 12th Street
between Avenues B & C

HOURS
April to October 31st
Sat – Sun: 11 a.m. – 4 p.m.
or when the gate is open

Votive candles and offerings in memory of Nugget, 1992-2016

The colors are vibrant, full of life and hope, but the message is somber. The climate is rapidly changing and it's time to take action. I notice a detail on the mural; a submarine named *S.S. Pollution* floating near a school of fish. Does anyone listen? Do people care?

A different day. Outside the garden's gate, I see a cluster of votive candles, a funerary wreath, and bouquets of wilted roses. A humble memorial to a young man, shot outside the garden. Who was he? So much death in one single block.

Left: 1. Clay angel 2. Halloween decorations 3. Seashells and beads 4. Children's mural about the environment
Right: Portrait of Nugget by muralist Antonio "Chico" Garcia

A month goes by, two. A mural appears, painted by the local artist Chico in memory of the young man. The mural reads: "Nugget, 1992-2016," followed by the dedication, "We're all a family under the stars."

It's summer now and the candles have been removed. The garden is bursting with blooming sunflowers. Volunteers clear the paths preparing for an evening performance with local musicians. I smile at the memory of the young man and the continuous cycle. Growth, pain, memory, and peace.

Left: Blooming sunflowers; Right: Stencil murals and paintings by neighborhood children

17

EL SOL BRILLANTE COMMUNITY GARDEN

When approaching El Sol Brillante, the first thing one notices is the wrought-iron fence, seemingly announcing a path to a small Palacio in Italy, or a villa in the south of France.

Created in 1993 by the sculptor and welder Julie Dermansky, the fence, titled *Garden of Earthy Delights*, has since become the neighborhood's best-known fixture. Distinguished and whimsical all at once, it features fleur-de-lys spikes rising to the sky and happy iron designs of flowers, plants, birds, dogs and even rats, nocturnal visitors to the garden.

There's an elegance to this garden and a sense of order. Trellised paths lead to hidden nooks and corners. Urns and small statues, strategically placed among the lots, catch one by surprise, like the marble eagle holding in his talons a coiled snake, or the urn split apart by the roots of a rose bush growing from within.

Forest mural by Jeramy Turner, 2019

WEBSITE:
http://elsolbrillante.org

ADDRESS
522 E. 12th Street
between Avenues A & B

HOURS
April to October 31st
Sat – Sun: Noon – Dusk
or when the gate is open

BY:
JULIE
DERMANSKY
1993

A wooden bucket overflowing with water brings images of tranquility; a broken head made out of limestone, his open mouth constantly feeding on rain and snow from the sky, enchants.

Founded in the late '70s, El Sol Brillante is one of the four community gardens that belongs to the "green corridor" of East 12th Street. The children and grandchildren of the founders and the many community volunteers are now the new members attending the grounds and showing visitors that such place can exist in the city.

Left: 1. Fence detail 2. Eagle statue holding a snake in its talons 3. Garden gate created in 1993 by Julie Dermansky 4. Limestone head rising from the earth; Right: Tiger lilies

A mural designed by Jeremy Turner was added in 2019, an homage to the plants, trees, and flowers, creating an extra dimension to the garden. Looking at the mural from a distance one hardly knows where the garden ends and imagination begins.

It is here that you can find shelter from the heat, as the outside world moves by with its cacophony. In the brilliant sun of this place, you can listen without being affected, as if all sound has been blocked by the cast-iron gate.

Left: Black-eyed Susans and coneflower; Right: Rose roots bursting out of urn

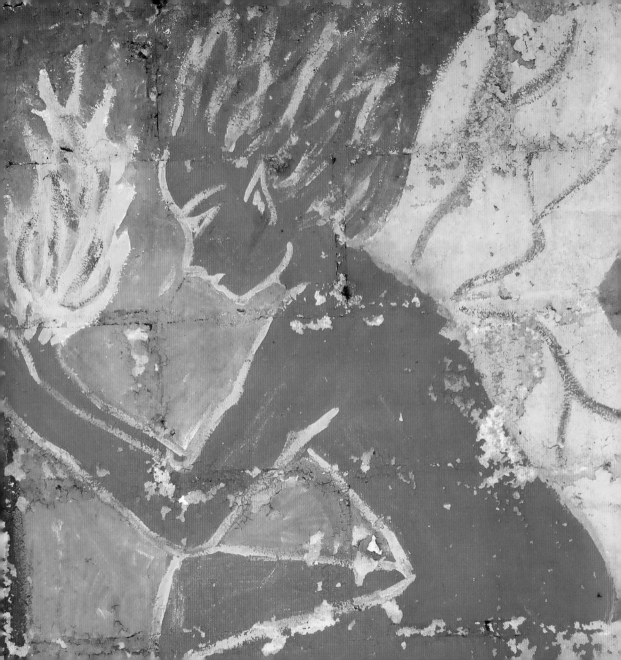

18

DIAS Y FLORES COMMUNITY GARDEN

Dias y Flores, or Days and Flowers, is named after a song written by the Cuban musician Silvio Rodriguez. A romantic song for sultry Caribbean nights, hardly fitting the "mood" expected in a drug-infested New York City neighborhood of the '70s.

Whimsical and yet profound, the garden speaks of years of activity and social conscience of people coming together to help those less fortunate, bringing hope and optimism to the neighborhood.

"Being accepted," that's what the garden was, and still is, all about, as one is welcomed by the sound of a banjo or the deep voice of a Shakespearean actor.

It's hard to imagine that before the garden this spot was home to an abandoned building used by gangs, junkies, and prostitutes. People came here to settle scores and often die, not to plant flowers.

WEBSITE:
diasyfloresgarden.wordpress.com

ADDRESS
E. 13th Street
between Avenues A & B

HOURS
April to October 31st
Sat – Sun: Noon – 5:00 p.m.
or when the gate is open

Young spirit holding fire

Then, in a story, a beautiful tradition, that repeats itself all across the East Village and Alphabet City, a group of local horticulturists and community volunteers, took it upon themselves to clear the lot.

These days the garden remains as spirited as at its inception, with colorful murals, a small stage, a solar-powered fountain, and a fishpond. Yoga, tai chi, and craft classes add a strong element of education to the garden. Haunted Halloween, Winter Solstice bonfire, and an end-of-season party make this garden the place to meet kindred spirits and celebrate life.

Left: Climate change painting; Right: 1. Growing tomatoes 2. Volunteers working in the garden 3. Sculpted head made of wood 4. Ripe tomatoes; Following page: Table decked for Halloween

WEST SIDE COMMUNITY GARDENS

1

THE GARDENS OF ST. LUKE IN THE FIELDS

If you don't know it's there, you might just miss it, walking past this secret garden's doorway, not knowing the natural peace on the other side of the brick walls.

In 1820, a small group of residents of the riverfront village of Greenwich, gathered together to organize an Episcopal church for their growing community. They named the church after St. Luke, the physician evangelist, in recognition of the village's role as a refuge from the yellow fever epidemics that plagued New York.

Since then, the garden has experienced a tremendous transformation, but still remains a hidden gem of the neighborhood. The tall brick wall overflowing with cascading greenery, and the cast-iron gate, entwined with foliage, plays tricks with the eyes, keeping people away, unaware of its beauty.

WEBSITE:
stlukeinthefields.org/about-us/our-gardens

ADDRESS
485 Hudson Street

HOURS
Mon – Sun: 10 a.m. – Dusk
The Gardens are closed on holidays.

Peonies and irises in full bloom

Once you enter, the garden fills you with a quiet strength. People stretched in comfortable benches listen to music, while others escape reality in the pages of a book. Intoxicating scents of blooming roses and peonies add more to the magic, as large hydrangeas and alliums sprout from the well-tended earth.

Everything is quiet and pristine, so it's not a wonder that hundreds of birds stop by in their migratory path. Adding twenty types of moths and butterflies, the garden proves to be a small miracle.

Left: Cast iron flower holder; Right: Garden grounds on a quiet afternoon

Yet, there's much more to be admired than just its beauty. In the '80s the AIDS Project of St. Luke's was founded, providing meals to tens of thousands of people in need, and furthering social justice. A beacon to the community, the church continues to play an active role in the lives of the poor and the disadvantaged, as well as functioning as a learning center in the neighborhood.

Pretty and peaceful, the garden embodies this same benevolence. Find the portal in the brick wall. Step through. You will be transported.

Blooming alliums and hydrangeas

2

LAGUARDIA CORNER GARDEN

The names of the roses go on and on, as do the intoxicating colors and scents: Alba White, Stanwell Perpetual, Charles Mallerin, Don Juan, Phloxy Baby, and Rosa Laxa. Madame Hardy—one of the most beautiful white roses ever bred, French Lace, Eglantyne, and Morden Blush are here, too.

I walk around mesmerized by the variety of roses. Amazingly, what was once a rat-infested lot in the mid-70s, is now one of the most important rose-breeding locations in the city.

As if the roses are not enough, one is dazzled by the display of daffodils, tulips, irises, peonies, and other perennials, as well as shrubs and fruit trees. A natural habitat for monarch butterflies and bees, the garden adds another dimension to the already oxygen-deprived city.

WEBSITE:
laguardiacornergarden.org/wp

ADDRESS
511 LaGuardia Place
between Bleecker &
Houston Streets

HOURS
April: Sat. & Sun. 2 p.m. – 6 p.m.
May: 10 a.m. – 6 p.m.
June – Aug: 10 a.m. – 8 p.m.
Sept & Oct: 10 a.m. – 6 p.m.

Blooming roses; the garden boasts one of the largest varieties of roses in the city

The tranquility however is not often easy to retain. Being in a prominent and coveted real-estate location, the garden had, and still has, to constantly fight for its survival. With New York University looming threateningly above the garden, the community is faced with the devastating possibility that the plot will be taken over by developers.

Strolling around on a sunlit evening, such thoughts vanish. Volunteers quietly attend their lots, as people, sitting on wooden chairs and benches, enjoy a moment away from their hectic schedule.

Left: Young woman walking among irises, foxglove, and alliums; Right: The garden bursting with color

Open from early spring to late fall, the garden offers numerous activities, classes and entertainment for both adults and children. Musical performances, poetry readings, birthday celebrations, and Halloween costume contests are a few of the many ways that the garden celebrates the seasons. The annual *Rose Walk*, is one activity not to be missed. It's a self-guided tour through the lots identifying and celebrating the existence of the abundant varieties of roses, and another example of the many paradoxes in the city's life.

Left: Tibetan flags and garden plot; Right: Blooming clematis; Following page: Rock Garden with whimsical creature

3

HELL'S KITCHEN FARM

A rooftop farm. A garden in the sky. Plants and vegetables sway gently in the wind amidst skyscrapers, billboards, and cranes. A tall apple tree, ripe with fruit, extends its branches towards the clouds. Kale, lettuce, spinach, and thyme grow in abundance inside blue kiddie pools tended by young volunteers.

The garden's history begins in 2010, when a team of neighborhood organizations, including the Clinton Housing Development Company, Rauschenbush Metro Ministries, and Metropolitan Community Church, brought their garden plan to life atop the Metro Baptist Church on 40th Street, just off 9th Avenue.

Their goal was to cultivate healthier food for the needy that frequent this gritty area around the Port Authority Bus Terminal.

WEBSITE:
hkfp.org

ADDRESS
410 W. 40th Street
Metro Baptist Church Rooftop

HOURS
Thu & Sat: 10 a.m. – 1 p.m.
weather permitting

Golden marigolds under imposing skyscrapers

I visited the garden on a cool summer morning, where young
volunteers tended the plants. Kay, a long-standing member, explained
the many challenges they had to face, such as complying with city
regulations for safety, carrying up piles of dirt and pebbles four
flights of steps, or fighting off pigeons feasting on the young seeds.

After trial and error, the gardeners realized that wire mesh
and netting keeps the birds away, a technique that continues
to work to this day, so that the garden can flourish and be enjoyed.

Left: Senior volunteer teaching the young; Right: 1. Welcome sign 2. A young volunteers on the task 3. Apple tree with skyscraper in the background 4. Young volunteer holding wire mesh

4

CLINTON COMMUNITY GARDEN

In the old rough and tumble area of Hell's Kitchen, the Clinton Garden is an unexpected place of respite. The garden is divided into two tranquil parts featuring winding paths and pleasing places to sit and muse. As so many other community gardens, this was an abandoned lot before residents and the city's Green Thumb program cleaned and cultivated it in the late '70s.

In 1981 when the city proposed putting the property up for auction, the gardeners formed the "Committee to Save Clinton Community Garden" and ran a "Square Inch Campaign," in which a $5.00 donation bought a piece of the garden.

The story attracted national attention in magazines, newspapers, and television, as well as the eventual personal support of Mayor Koch, who bought the first square inch of the garden.

WEBSITE:
Under construction

ADDRESS
434 W. 48th Street
between 10th & 9th Avenues

HOURS
Sat – Sun: 9 a.m. – 6 p.m.
or when the gate is open

Coneflowers reflected on a small water basin

Today an average of 500–600 people use the garden during the summer, and over 2,000 people have access to keys. The garden's programs include an annual Summer Solstice event, potluck dinners, art shows, weddings, music performances, gardening seminars, dance recitals, and even fashion photo-shoots.

Clinton Community Garden is literally a rescued space, a reclaiming of urban blight, making it bright, making it grow, and giving it back to both residents and passersby.

Left: Tool shed; Right: Variety of plants in the Native American garden; Following page: Section of remaining mural depicting a worm, by Mallory Abramson, prominent garden founder and community leader

Garlic Chives
Allium tuberosum

Peppermint
Mentha piperita

Spearmint
Mentha spicata

5

OASIS COMMUNITY GARDEN

A sandy beach surrounded by purple and white Adirondack chairs; a bathtub filled with rainwater amidst tiger lilies; a marble bench supported by lion heads; mannequin dolls hanging upside down wearing "I Love NY" t-shirts, and elfish creatures peeking through the willow's branches. This artful mélange challenges the visitor to find out the story behind these creations.

The Oasis has been part of the neighborhood for the last forty years. Once a barren lot filled with drug paraphernalia and garbage, it was hardly a safe place to walk by, and of course, never a place to linger after dusk.

After the garden was cleared of debris, a "sand beach" was created in an attempt to give the neighborhood children the illusion of being by the sea.

WEBSITE:
oasiscommunitygarden.com

ADDRESS
W. 52nd Street
between 11th & 10th Avenues

HOURS
Tue: Noon – 2 p.m.
Wed & Fri:* 6 p.m. – 8 p.m.
(*June, July & August Only)
Sat – Sun: Noon – 4 p.m.

Stainless-steel sculpture reflecting the buildings across the garden

The bathtub, once overflowing with koi, functioned as a small "aquarium." After a break in the structure, the water leaked out and the fish died, but the bathtub remains looking for a new life.

I sit on a bench observing a group of children running around, while the parents enjoy a quiet evening. The children remind me of my sister and me in Greece, playing with our friends by the river bank.

I'm confident that the moments that these children share with one another, will one day grow into lasting friendships.

Left: Vegetable garden and tool shed; Right: 1. Detail of a lion head 2. Wet earth 3. Adirondack chairs 4. Cactus and pebbles
Following page: Sand, Adirondack chairs, and bathtub recreating the feel of a sandy beach

6

WEST 87TH STREET PARK & GARDEN

This quiet place in the heart of the Upper West Side provides calm in a city that never sleeps. A blooming trumpet vine entwined around the garden's gate welcomes you. Ivy cascading from the adjacent building transforms the spot into a green fortress. A large umbrella offers shelter from the sun, while a children's corner filled with toys and bicycles occupies the littlest visitors. A young couple leans over and kisses, while further away two elderly women bask in the sunlight. White lilies bloom everywhere.

The calm and the lush greenery on this gorgeous summer evening, make me feel melancholic, almost nostalgic, for something that I can't define. I walk around the paths thinking that beauty such as this should be shared, and that everybody should experience these small city havens.

WEBSITE:
Unavailable

ADDRESS
55 W. 87th Street
between Central Park West
& Columbus Avenue

HOURS
Sat – Sun: Noon – 4 p.m.
or when the gate is open

Chairs under trellis

A man and his wife greet me. "Do you like our garden?" they ask. "We've lived in the neighborhood for years; you should have seen how bad this place used to be."

I want to tell them how unexpected all this harmony is, and how much beauty and knowledge I've absorbed by walking through the different neighborhoods... but I stop. There's so much to convey, I fear I'll be at a loss for words, and besides, the garden says it much better than any of us ever could.

Left: Glorious ivy; Right: 1. Snow-white lilies 2. Children's corner 3. People under white umbrella 4. Cascading trumpet vines

7

WEST SIDE COMMUNITY GARDEN

In 1976, local residents turned this trash-strewn vacant lot on Columbus Avenue into a garden. Then, miraculously, all involved parties – the community board, developers, and the New York City Planning Commission – agreed that this beautiful spot should become a permanent garden.

Today the garden includes a "floral amphitheater," public seating and serene spots of relaxation. The garden's design is award-winning and the flower plots dazzle. The plots are maintained by garden members and volunteers whose love and care is evident in the smallest of details.

Most of the herbs and flowers are from seeds sown in the greenhouse at the majestic St. John the Divine. So everything seems blessed and right.

WEBSITE:
westsidecommunitygarden.org

ADDRESS
123 W. 89th Street
between Amsterdam &
Columbus Avenues

HOURS
Sat – Sun: Noon – 4 p.m.
or when the gate is open

People enjoying a flute concert in the garden's amphitheater

Two-thirds of the property is devoted to flowers and one third to vegetables and herbs. There are also community compost bins by the "Compost Gate" where neighbors may deposit their coffee grounds and other vegetable waste. River birches, and Chinese cedar trees flank the sides, adding another layer of beauty to the garden.

For me, the serenity of the garden was encapsulated in a cool summer evening, when people gathered to listen to a flute concert. In rapt attention, all sat mesmerized, as the fading light bid goodbye.

Left: 1. Community garden banner 2-3. Private lots 4. Women listening to concert in summer attire; Right: Vegetable lot

8

LOTUS GARDEN

I'm standing outside this garden on a beautiful spring evening. The gate is locked because it's past visitor's hours, but I'm waiting for Jeff Kindley, a garden member, to appear with the key.

I met Jeff a few weeks before when I first visited this hidden gem. His enthusiasm for the garden and the neighborhood were so inspiring that I wanted to return and experience it all again.

Located on the roof of the parking garage of the Columbia Condominiums, this 7,000-square-foot urban oasis is often missed not only because of its discreet entrance, but also because people seldom lift their heads to look up.

Once, two old movie theaters, the Riverside and Riviera, used to stand on this spot. When they closed, the building fell into disrepair and was demolished, leaving an empty lot.

WEBSITE:
thelotusgarden.org/wp

ADDRESS
250 W. 97th Street
between Broadway &
West End Avenue

HOURS
April to November 15th
Sun: 1 p.m. – 4 p.m.
or when the gate is open

Serpentine-like pear tree

Thankfully, a collaboration took place among the new developer,
William Zeckendorf Jr., and community activists Carrie Maher,
a horticulturist, and Mark Greenwald, an architect. A set of stairs from
the street to the soon-to-be green roof was built, soil was lifted
up high by a cherry picker, followed by the installation of two fish ponds,
and the planting of fruit trees, that are still tended by local residents.

Green space can still be found in this dense city, and lotuses can
rise from parking garages.

Left: Pond with koi; Right: 1. Blooming lilies 2. Statue of water carrier 3. Roses 4. Pear tree and blooming azelias
Following page: Garden grounds above parking lot overlooking the street

EAST HARLEM COMMUNITY GARDENS

1. Humacao Community Garden

2. Herb Garden

3. East Harlem Community Garden

4. Anonymous

5. El Gallo Community Garden

6. Jackie Robinson Community Garden

7. Carver Community Garden

8. Dream Street Park

HUMACAO COMMUNITY GARDEN

Apples and peaches and cherries. "Have one!" Miriam says, picking an apple from the tree and handing it to me. "It's a good season this year, but once they drop on the ground nobody wants them." The apple is still bitter but sumptuous.

I walk with Miriam around the garden commenting on how beautiful everything looks. "In some neighborhoods, rich people move in, clean up the lots, and put up shiny benches. It's all good and all, but they destroy the character," she complains.

Miriam exudes confidence. "This is Casper," she introduces me to a little poodle, "Make sure you include him in the book. And this alligator, my daughter and I made it." She points to a two-foot-long mythical creature painted deep phosphorescent green, with a red sock for a tongue.

Miriam holding a bucket with apples

WEBSITE:
Unavailable

ADDRESS
333 E. 108th Street
between 2nd & 1st Avenues

HOURS
When the gate is open

Blue plastic balls of all sizes hang from the trees, Miriam's newly created universe. "I wanted to commemorate the Apollo landing, but now I think I'm going to keep them."

I walk to the small altar with the traditional Madonna holding a young Jesus. I had first noticed the altar earlier this winter when the garden was covered in snow and the gate locked.

"This is Caridad del Cobre," the patroness and guardian of all sailors," Miriam explains as if reading my thoughts.

Left: Crocodile made out of garden materials, tongue made out of red sock; Right: 1. Fabric flowers in vase. 2. Found poster commemorating Apollo's landing on the moon 3. Rock garden 4. "Caridad del Cobre," Madonna of sailors

Images of my father pass before me. Did he ever encounter this Madonna in his travels, and did she ease the squals and storms?

Legend speaks of two Spanish captains heading for the New World, along with two Native American brothers, and an African slave child. While at sea, a storm arose, threatening their tiny boat. Juan, the child, was wearing a medal with the image of the Virgin Mary. They began to pray, when the apparition of the Virgin Mary appeared holding young Jesus on her left arm and a gold cross in her right, leading them to safety.

"Planets" made out of plastic balls

"Come let me show you my rock garden," Miriam calls.

Her geniality is boundless, like the apples of the tree that keep growing in abundance. She tells me that she used to play in this lot as a young child. "My mother used to call me from this window," she points to the adjacent building and then to the sky.

Miriam, the name of the Madonna, another reincarnation of the Virgin Mary. Eternal, humble, and always found nearby when you least expect her.

Traditional "casita" with raised platform and curious objects

2

HERB GARDEN

In the urban environment, a plot between two apartment buildings is both an oasis and meeting ground. The Herb Garden on East 111th Street, a product of the nonprofit New York Restoration Project, (NYRP) is such a wellspring.

Who started NYRP? None other than the beloved Bette Midler. Deeply involved in the arts and the welfare of the community, she delivered with actions when others stood by watching neighborhood after neighborhood being destroyed.

Since its creation, NYRP has been pivotal to the survival of many community gardens throughout the five boroughs of Manhattan. In the '90s, when the city was considering selling the plots to real estate developers, the organization stepped in and bought a great number of these gardens and so rescuing them.

From the garden to the table

WEBSITE:
nyrp.org/green-spaces/garden-details/herb-garden

ADDRESS
176 E. 111th Street
between Lexington
& 3rd Avenues

HOURS
Tue: Noon – 1 p.m.
Wed: 9 a.m. – 11 a.m. /
6 p.m. – 7 p.m.
Thu: 8 a.m. – 10 a.m. /
2 p.m. – 3:30 p.m.
Fri: 3 p.m. – 8 p.m.
Sat: 10 a.m. – 11 a.m.
Sun: 9 a.m. – 11 a.m. /
3 p.m. – 8 p.m.

The NYRP now owns and manages fifty-two community gardens. Famous artists, performers, fashion designers, and large chain stores have subsequently contributed, making sure that these unique spaces lack nothing.

The residents, in return, keep these spaces well tended, to an almost pristine state. When not working their plots, they gather together for barbecues or meetings, surrounded by tomatoes, basil, peppers, and parsley. City life can wait. The garden is here for all.

Left: The garden in full bloom; Right: 1. Herb garden 2. Birthday party 3. Plots after the rain 4. Spring tones

3

EAST HARLEM COMMUNITY GARDEN

Spring. The garden feels abandoned, as if the earth, in this part of Harlem, forgot to bear any flowers. A mural of the Castillo and Lady Liberty covers the back wall, reminders of perhaps, happier days. The paint is peeling, like much else in this garden, yet there's strength in this emptiness.

Two children, jackets thrown on the ground, fight over a bicycle with a rusty frame. A man, perhaps their uncle or their father, works on the earth, lost in his thoughts. Everyone seeming to keep an observer's distance in this frozen landscape.

June 18th, the Puerto Rican Day Parade. East Harlem vibrates with color and music. People stroll out onto the streets enjoying the sun and a good barbecue. In contrast to the winter months and early spring, the garden feels alive.

WEBSITE:
Unavailable

ADDRESS
433 E. 117th Street
Lexington & Third Avenues

HOURS
When the gate is open

"Jardin de Manati;" mural commemorating famed town in Puerto Rico

A group of men in baseball hats, short sleeves and sunglasses, play dominoes. A little farther away a group of women, mothers, grandmothers, and grandchildren, coquettishly pose for the camera. A small boy, the same boy I had seen months ago riding his bicycle, runs over to greet me. He's warm and affectionate, welcoming me like another member of the family. I look back at the wall. Lady Liberty caught in a beam of sunlight. One nation, under God, with grace and tolerance. The gestures and language of a garden.

Left: Neighbors enjoying a summer barbecue; Right: Madonna and young supplicant; Following page: Children playing before mural with Puerto Rican flag

4

ANONYMOUS

A place so poignant it steals your breath away. A fence surrounding an empty lot. The sign reads: "Out of respect to those who lost their lives on March 12, 2014, please do not deface this wall with graffiti."

Harlem 2014. A Spring day. Eight people, eight neighbors, unaware that these were to be their last moments. Eight people, at different stages of their lives, with different hopes and dreams: Griselde Camacho, 44; Carmen Tanco, 67; Rosaura Hernandez, 22; Andreas Panagopoulos, 43; Rosaura Barrios Vazquez, 43; Alexis Salas, 22; and George Amadeo, 44. The eighth victim was never identified.

The gas explosion was so powerful that it was described as if it had been an earthquake. Two buildings collapsed

WEBSITE:
Unavailable

ADDRESS
Lexington Avenue
between E. 116th – E. 117th Streets

Flowers in memory of the eight who perished in a gas explosion

and seventy victims were brought to the hospital, among them a boy
with a burned back and a woman with a broken neck.

Since then, the rubble has been removed and the lots cleared,
but the eight people are never forgotten, their photographs posted
on the fence. Each holiday neighbors and family stop by to place
flowers or birthday balloons in their memory. The victims' eyes are
never accusatory, just sad for living and dying in unsafe conditions,
the price of being poor and disadvantaged in this city of wealth.

Left: Sign asking to respect the lot; Right: Flowers and small offerings; Following page: Balloons for a birthday celebration that never came

5

EL GALLO COMMUNITY GARDEN

The grandmother sways her arms, pointing to a plot of lettuce. The boys try to pay attention, but all they want to do is run around and play amidst the flowers. The grandmother remains firm and holds their attention. The boys chuckle. They know that I'm photographing them, so they break into wide smiles.

Their mother, a young woman in her early twenties, is rocking a baby carriage under a large umbrella, chatting with a friend. Another quiet evening in the neighborhood in this safe place salvaged from harder times.

"I try to teach them respect for the earth, but their minds are always in their games," the grandmother says. She walks around with me, proudly showing off her blooming hydrangeas. "Once there was nothing here but rubble and look at it now!"

WEBSITE:
Unavailable

ADDRESS
1895 Lexington Avenue
between E. 117th – E. 118th Streets

HOURS
When the gate is open

Undulating circles and colors

Like so many other gardens in Hispanic Harlem, El Gallo features the perfect casita, with window sills painted in blue-green Caribbean colors and doorways in bright yellows and pinks. Windmills, old scarecrows, and wishing wells are hidden in the foliage adding more flair to this whimsical place.

"We can't wait for Halloween," one of the boys tells me. "You must come back, we even have a costume contest."

Their grandmother smiles. The garden overflows with pride.

Left: Local gardener teaching young children about planting and composting; Right: Community plots; Following page: Garden details

6

JACKIE ROBINSON COMMUNITY GARDEN

A freezing cold winter wind sweeps down Park Avenue. The streets are deserted as East Harlem shivers. Through the fence, I see bouquets of colorful flowers, blue-green, orange, and purple, in striking contrast with the barren earth. These flowers never wither and never drop their blooms, not withstanding, like the community, time and the elements. Made out of fabric or plastic they stoically accept the wind and the rain.

The garden is asking to be seen, to be explored, but I'm cold and it has started to rain, so I walk away.

Then it's summer again at Jackie Robinson. The plots are ripe, overflowing with vegetables and herbs. The fake flowers are still standing, and new ones have been added, creating a world of clashing colors.

"Open air" living room with mirror, table, and chairs

WEBSITE:
Unavailable

ADDRESS
103 E. 122nd Street between Park & Lexington Avenues

HOURS
When the gate is open

At the end of the garden, a tree functions as an art gallery, its trunk decorated from top to bottom with old paintings. Faded photographs of famous boxers and athletes cover the surrounding walls, another special touch of those who tend it.

A group of neighbors relaxes under the small gazebo. They laugh and tease each other. There's an openness in this garden that I find endearing. The neighborhood is poor but the spirit of the people is as large as the sky.

Left: Tree Gallery; Right: 1. Spirited garden volunteers 2. Plastic and fabric flowers 3. Vegetable plot 4. Outdoor gallery in orange hues

7

CARVER COMMUNITY GARDEN

Tucked away on East 124th street, this lovely spot can be easily missed, not because it's not important, but because of its geographical distance from the rest of the gardens.

Since its inception, the garden has been through some rough times, and has been twice threatened to be demolished for a new development.

Part of the neighborhood for the past eleven years, the garden was once used as an open daycare center for children, but lack of funding and the unsafe conditions of some of the garden's structures forced the classes to be canceled.

But the spirit of the volunteers endured. They kept digging and planting vegetables and flowers, creating a beautifully maintained space for all to share.

WEBSITE:
Unavailable

ADDRESS
242 E. 124th Street
between 3rd & 2nd Avenues

HOURS
When the gate is open

Mural with hummingbird and flowers

Walking in the garden one feels humbled by the many struggles the community has been faced with. The grounds speak of care and commitment. Everything is well thought out but the underlying message that everything is ephemeral is not lost.

A colorful mural of a hummingbird resting on a branch catches my attention. Butterflies float around intercepted by plants and flowers. What is real and what is an imaginary extension?

This garden seems to obliterate all physical boundaries.

Left: Gazebo with black eye Susans; Right: Community plots

8

DREAM STREET PARK

I heard the man on the bench talking to his demons, his hands flagellating in the air, body twisting, and kicking. He screamed, then reclined on the bench, exhausted from his battle. Released.

Like a shaman diving into the depths of the earth breathing smoke and fire in search of answers, his journey is long and arduous. If he survives, he'll bring back healing; if not, he'll remain a prisoner of the spirit world and "her" power.

Ezili, is a goddess of tremendous potency, deeply rooted in the Haitian and Caribbean cultures. Protector and avenger, she's tender like the first light of dawn, and cruel like Hades.

This garden is still her sacred ground, a reminder of times past, but not forgotten. A gate with a bright red heart melted on the fence separates dream from reality. Dare to enter?

WEBSITE:
Unavailable

ADDRESS
225 E. 124th Street
between 3rd & 2nd Avenues

HOURS
Weekly: 7 a.m. – 7 p.m.

Heart shaped entrance gate

According to the community elders, the heart represents Ezili's *veve*, a sacred symbol identifying her presence. Some say that back in time the grounds were used for performing rituals, others insist that the heart is a symbol of love, and that the rest are just silly tales.

I cross the gate, realizing that the path, now overgrown with weeds, is also shaped like a heart. Coincidence? The truth is somewhere in between. A mural, the length of three adjacent buildings and painted in bright colors, rises above me.

Left: Flower beds with mural in the background; Right: Cut-out figures reated by community children

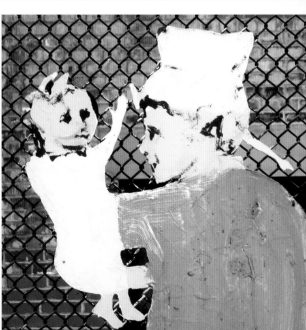

It represents the world, with people leaving Africa, "dancing" their way across to Central America in search of a better life.

The mural was painted in 1995 by a group of homeless teenagers led by Creative Artworks, a non-profit, non-partisan coalition of the arts. The lower parts were painted by the youngest children, while the middle and the top sections by more seasoned artists.

The homeless man stirs. I want to walk closer to him, but I keep my distance. Today Ezili is kind to him, and I don't want to disturb her.

Left: Frankenstein; Right: Names of artists and volunteers led by Creative Artworks Coalition; Following page: World mural, 1995

WEST HARLEM COMMUNITY GARDENS

1. West 104th Street Garden

2. La Perla Community Garden

3. Mobilization For Change Community Garden

4. The Joseph Daniel Wilson Memorial Gardens

5. New 123rd Street Block Association Garden

6. West 132nd Street Garden

7. Harlem Grown 134th Street Green House

8. Hope Stevens Community Garden

9. Frank White Memorial Garden

10. Friendship Garden (Wicked)

11. Convent Garden

12. Hope: The Friendly Garden on the Hill

13. William A. Harris Garden

14. Morris Jumel Community Garden

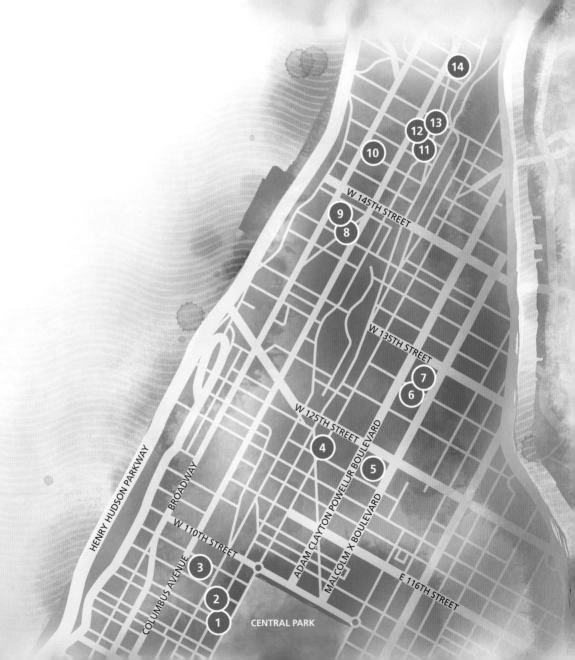

1

WEST 104TH STREET GARDEN

On the Upper West Side nearby Columbia University, two gardens stand next to each other like sisters, competing for affection. One delicate and artistic, her sky-blue gazebo matching the clouds, the other practical and down to earth, with rows of vegetable plots. Interchangeable. Sharing everything. Witnessing the stories and the transformation of the neighborhood, and the great efforts made to restore this land into a habitable place.

After the first plots were cleared, a huge infestation of rodents followed, making it impossible to plant anything. The poisons used to eradicate the rats only exacerbated the problem, with the plants dying and the rats happily going about building their nests.

Desperate for a solution, a volunteer suggested introducing cats to the gardens, and the rest is history.

WEBSITE:
west104garden.org

ADDRESS
8 W. 104th Street
between Central Park West
& Amsterdam Avenue

HOURS
April to October 31st
Sat – Sun: 10 a.m. – 4 p.m.
or when the gate is open

Birthday party under sky-blue gazebo

With an insulated straw-lined house, and plenty of food to hunt, the cats became an integral feature of the gardens.

Walking around these sisters, it's hard to miss the care invested by the volunteers, from keeping meticulously clean paths, to organizing plant sales, and seasonal activities.

But for me, it's the tranquility and the sense of someone always watching that make all the difference, as myriad cat eyes follow my every step through the foliage; the perfect "solitary" companions.

Left: Watering cans; Right: Garden sign painted by volunteers

2

LA PERLA COMMUNITY GARDEN

A hard-scrabble plot filled with garbage, soothed over time with love and care, can transform into a pearl, an alluring garden, just a stone's throw to the west of Central Park. Tiny flags undulate in the wind, accompanied by the subtle sound of seashells and chimes, as mirrors hanging from tree branches reflect the light, play tricks with the eyes.

A mural created by neighborhood children decorates the western wall. Splashes of red and yellow are still visible from an older painting, proof of the ever changing life of the garden.

A man with a long beard, smoking an unfiltered cigarette and reading the *New Yorker*, welcomes me. Sitting on an Adirondack chair before a wooden stage, one could confuse him for a Shakespearean actor, or maybe King Lear himself.

WEBSITE:
Unavailable

ADDRESS
76 W. 105th Street
between Manhattan
& Columbus Avenues

HOURS
When the gate is open

Sculpture made of marble from St. John the Divine; artist unknown

His name is Robert and indeed he is from England. When I ask him about the sculpture standing at the entrance of the garden, he tells me that all he knows is that the marble was brought from St. John the Divine, the inspiring Gothic church nearby, which ennobles this corner of the city.

I look at the sculpture, my mind drifting to the sublime Cycladic figures soaking up the Aegean light; perfect and mysterious, like this mysterious statue.

Left: 1. Murals painted by local children 2. Flags and garlands left over from a July 4th celebration 3. Robert enjoying a quiet evening
Right: Garden at dusk

3

MOBILIZATION FOR CHANGE COMMUNITY GARDEN

Mobilization for Change Community Garden is small but intriguing, filled with all kinds of whimsical objects; a young Buddha seated in a child's wooden chair amidst Hindu deities; an outdoor fireplace festooned with a gigantic wreath and candles, a necklace tossed by a flower pot, all brought together under the aegis of a gigantic blue umbrella.

And then I see her, the Gypsy Queen of my childhood stories, bust turned sideways and torso covered in cherry blossoms. A stream of sunlight catches the gold coins in her hair. Her green eyes are pensive, and her face filled with cracks.

In what dream world is she traveling now, reading beginnings and endings on a palm? How many nights has she danced around fires, where children toss silver coins to the stars and dogs howl?

WEBSITE:
Unavailable

ADDRESS
995 Columbus Avenue

HOURS
April to October 31st
Mon – Fr: 9 a.m. – 9 p.m.
Sat – Sun: 9 a.m. – 5 p.m.
or when the gate is open

"Lady Luck" with enchanting green eyes amidst scattered blooms

Here in this quiet part of Harlem, I never thought that I'd encounter her, but then again it couldn't have been any other way; magic breeds magic. These gardens are a reflection of us.

Frame after frame I try to capture her beauty, but she evades me. The local women sitting on the bench call her Lady Luck. I call her Gypsy Queen, Aphrodite of Melos, and the Madonna of Guadalupe. I call her the four corners of the world coming together in this quaint garden, the true Delphic oracle.

Left: "Outdoor" fire place, Christmas wreath, and Lady Luck; Right: Small corners in the garden created by community members
Following page: Buddha child in repose

4

THE JOSEPH DANIEL WILSON MEMORIAL GARDEN

Murmurs captured in the leaves and eyes everywhere. The wind picks up speed, yet everything around me is engulfed in silence as if time has stopped forever. The garden is so lush and so pristine that you feel you've just entered a primeval forest dense with exotic plants and flowers.

I sit on a small bench. There is depth in this garden, a certain aura that draws you within. If I close my eyes I may be pulled into this world forever and become one with the invisible spirits.

A beautiful gate created by the sculptor Steven Schmerfeld adds another layer of isolation, or is it protection, from the outside world. Everything is possible here. All you have to do is dream and the forest nymphs will grant your wishes.

WEBSITE:
projectharmonynyc.org

ADDRESS
219 W. 122nd Street
between Frederick Douglas &
Adam Clayton Powell Jr. Blvds

HOURS
April to October 31st
or when the gate is open

Early spring in the garden

This magical place was founded by Joseph Daniel Wilson, an elderly Guyanese homeowner with a profound understanding of the earth and all natural things, a group of teens from the neighborhood, and Cindy Nibbelink, a writer and teacher.

In 1985, Cindy and her husband, Haja Worley, established Project Harmony, a grassroots, volunteer-driven nonprofit. With the help of other volunteers they cleaned fifty vacant lots all around Harlem, creating natural habitats for birds and native plants.

Left: 1. Tool shed decorated with butterflies and lizards 2. Wooden bridge 3. Cindy Worley, one of the garden's founders 4. Metal flamingo
Right: Mother Earth clay figurine hidden in the foliage

The same volunteers also introduced the Doers Cottage Industry and Environmental Program, helping people find apartments, start their own small businesses and furthering their education.

I was fortunate to meet Cindy on one of my visits, quietly working in a small plot. Her welcoming words and presence made me think of all these extraordinary people who've dedicated themselves so we can enjoy this beauty. This earth is alive and Mr. Wilson is still watching over his beloved garden.

Left: Hidden pond; Right: Photographs of live performances and children's messages to save the garden from gentrification
Following page: Dancing forest nymph

5

NEW 123RD STREET BLOCK ASSOCIATION GARDEN

I've walked for hours and hours in this historic neighborhood of New York City, the names of the streets calling out hope and struggle and justice; Frederick Douglass, Malcolm X, Marcus Garvey, and I'm grateful to have found such a welcoming place of respite.

There are no people around, just me and the blossoming trees, but the care and love for the garden are evident everywhere. Tidy plots and paths lead past a small ledge where tools are kept and an ornate trellis stands, waiting for the weight of summer grapes.

It's hard to believe that in 2012 this very same garden was buried under tons of rubble when the adjacent building collapsed. Nothing was left but debris and hundreds of questions about the unsafe conditions. Luckily no one was hurt, a small miracle in a community that has already endured so much.

WEBSITE:
west123street.org
Under Construction

ADDRESS
120 W. 123rd Street
between Adam Clayton Powell Jr.
& Malcolm X Blvds

HOURS
April to October 31st
or when the gate is open

Bright yellow and orange tulips under gray sky

The sky turns gray and there's a threat of rain. Everything about this garden is a big circle, and I'm a part of it. The church's tall tower looming over the garden adds another layer of spirituality and peace.

It's raining hard now, so I walk away, promising to return. A few blocks away I realize that I've lost my garden list. Just like that, gone with the wind. My first reaction is to get upset, but then I grow calmer. Perhaps it's better this way, with no compass, trusting only my instinct, in the true spirit of adventure.

Left: Well-maintained plots; Right: The garden's many faces

6

WEST 132ND STREET BLOCK ASSOCIATION GARDEN

The man watering the small flower plot smiles and waves. His disposition is quiet like this refuge. "You've just missed the young volunteers," he tells me. "They're all children and teenagers from the neighborhood. You'll be surprised how knowledgeable and committed they are to this garden."

I look around me, taking in the beauty. Everything feels bright, exuberant. I stop by the pond where water lilies bloom. Koi float around, their red and golden scales undulating in the morning light. Beautifully maintained paths meander around the garden, passed wooden benches and chairs, blooming clematis and catmint.

At the end of the garden, a tree catches my attention; its trunk is sleek, smooth to the touch, almost exotic. I could imagine such a tree growing somewhere in Hawaii or the Caribbean, but not here.

Crepe myrtle tree

WEBSITE:
Unavailable

ADDRESS
114 W. 132nd Street
between Adam Clayton Powell Jr.
& Malcolm X (Lenox) Blvds

HOURS
April to October 31st
or when the gate is open

"This is a crepe myrtle. You must come back in summer when it's in full bloom. The colors vary from deep purple to red with almost every shade in between," the man explains.

I return two more times. The garden is greener, lusher, but the tree continues to withhold its blooms.

"You're still too early," the same man smiles.

He reminds me of my grandfather in Greece. "Always so impatient," he used to tell me.

Left: Clematis, pansies, and bluebells; Right: Pond with water lilies and koi

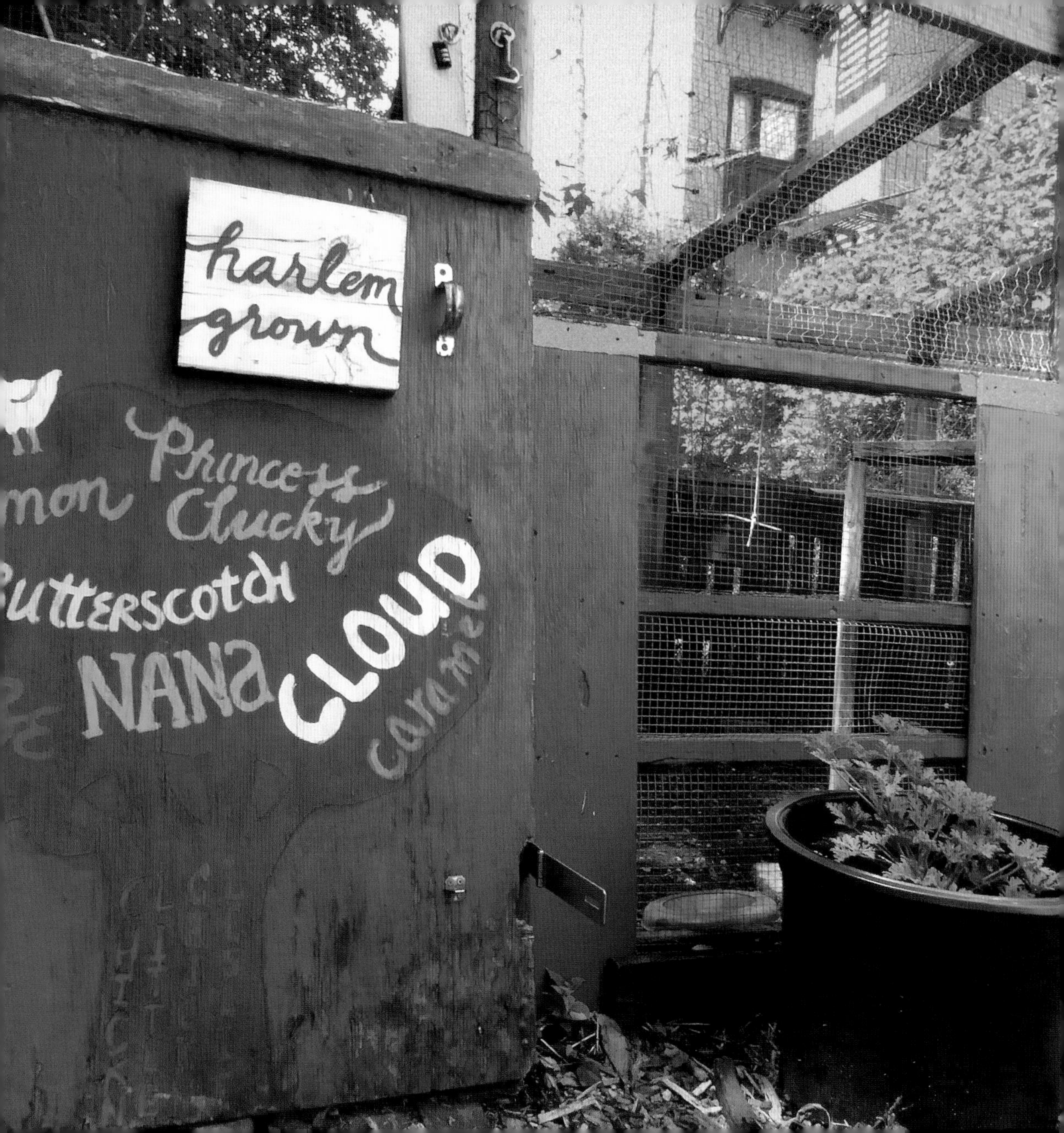
harlem grown
Princess
Clucky
NANA
CLOUD
caramel

7

HARLEM GROWN 134TH STREET GREEN HOUSE

Two youthful faces with wide-open eyes and orange t-shirts showcasing the Harlem Grown logo welcome me.

"Would you buy some vegetables? They're all from our garden," they say in unison.

Inside young men and women are busy, clearing plots and planting new seeds. It's volunteer day and the garden undulates with activity. There's food, face painting and drawing for the young as adults walk around discussing strategy and which parts of the garden need more tending. Colorful signs identify vegetables and herbs, another form of education for all those present.

Children run around a startling red chicken coop painted with sunflowers. The children try to draw the chickens' attention but the chickens are oblivious, the true "owners" of the garden.

WEBSITE:
http://www.harlemgrown.org/

ADDRESS
118 W. 134th Street
between Adam Clayton Powell Jr.
& Malcolm X Blvds

HOURS
April to October 31st
or when the gate is open

Colorful chicken coop

The expanding nonprofit Harlem Grown is all about education, teaching local kids how to live healthier lives through urban farming, sustainability, and nutrition. Another way Harlem Grown is fulfilling its mission is by raising support to renovate the many abandoned lots that remain in Harlem.

Currently, the organization has created eleven urban agriculture facilities ranging from soil-based farms, hydroponic greenhouses, and school gardens. How extraordinary is that? In the heart of the city.

Left: Young volunteers welcoming visitors; Right: Greenhouse; Following page: Herbs, vegetable and homegrown signs

8

HOPE STEVENS COMMUNITY GARDEN

I stop, drawing my breath. This garden is small, lacking the variety of flowers of other gardens, but the mural decorating the north wall steals my heart away. The brush strokes are powerful, bold, luminous. They attract the eye with such force, they obliterate everything else around it.

A trumpeter, in a sky-blue suit and hat, heralds a mother and child to mass, while further away two young girls, under a laced umbrella, enjoy a quiet moment in the park.

The mural, *Homage to Seurat: La Grande Jatte in Harlem,* inspired by Seurat's famous painting, *A Sunday Afternoon on the Island of La Grande Jatte,* is the only remaining New York City work by Eva Cockcroft, the prominent artist and leader of the community mural movement of the '60s.

"Homage to Seurat: La Grande Jatte in Harlem," by artist Eva Cockcroft, 1985

WEBSITE:
Unavailable

ADDRESS
505 W. 142nd Street &
Amsterdam Avenue

HOURS
April to October 31st
or when the gate is open

By 2007 the mural fell into serious disrepair. Portions of it were hastily covered with stucco to contain cracks and leaks from the adjacent building. The vibrant colors that once lit the neighborhood, were faded to pastels following the fate of so many other murals that once adorned Harlem.

That's when Rescue Public Murals, a national program founded in 2006 to preserve community artwork, stepped in. Working with meticulous care they brought the mural back to life.

Left: Artwork on the fence representing the community's many facets; Right "Homage to Seurat: La Grande Jatte in Harlem," detail

As I walk admiring the work, I notice a group of people consoling a man. His daughter, just twenty seven years old, was killed by a hit-and-run driver a few steps from the garden, and now the community has gathered to plant an apple tree in her memory. A small plaque has been placed at the foot of the tree, reading: "Planted in loving memory of Erica Imbasciani, July 6, 1992–March 22, 2019. Rooted in love, always in our hearts." It's hard to imagine the pain, a life lost, but not the young woman's spirit, now deeply rooted in the neighborhood.

"Homage to Seurat: La Grande Jatte in Harlem." The mural was restored in 2006 by Rescue Public Murals organization
Following page: Panoramic view

9

FRANK WHITE MEMORIAL GARDEN

Color, color everywhere. Exuberant, expanding, unafraid of being. Life bursting forward. Encountering this garden is like encountering the spirit of the entire neighborhood.

A group of elder men and women sitting outside the gate greet me. They are friendly but watchful. They continue their conversation but they never lose sight of me. They've never seen me before so they assess my intentions until they relax.

The boldness of this garden is unparalleled. Not a single spot has been left unpainted, from benches, to old tires, to flower pots and stone bricks marked with the neighborhood children's hand-prints, a modern Lascaux cave in the middle of Harlem.

A stage draped with fabrics stands in the back of the garden, near sheetrock panels painted with nature themes and poetry verses.

WEBSITE:
brotherhood-sistersol.org/programs/
environmental-program

ADDRESS
506 W. 143th Street between
Broadway & Amsterdam Avenue

HOURS
April to October 31st
or when the gate is open

Entrance to the garden, with performance stage in the distance

What makes this garden so unique is the tightly knit community that is run by the neighborhood's elders. They are the ones who watch over the premises, making sure that nobody misbehaves; adults and children alike. The sidewalk in front of the garden's gate is their extended living room where tournaments of Pinochle, card games and even an occasional barbecue take place. They know everybody's name and lineage and often function as advisors or mediators.

Left: Colorful flower pots; Right: Activities for the young by The Brotherhood/SisterSol organization

ESCAPE THE GARDEN: Challenge Course

INFO SHEET

Frank White Memorial Garden is a unique garden with a strong youth friendly space where young people love to be in. One of the attraction to our garden from groups and schools is because we have a Challenge Course, where teams and groups can come together to complete a challenge course where it brings the youth crew closer together.

ESCAPE THE GARDEN

CLUE #6
CHECKPOINT!!

Each member of your team must get across the rock wall, with NO falls. If one member of the group touches the ground, the whole team must start over.

Once your whole team has gotten across, you can pick up your next clue at the gazebo.

The garden is dedicated to the memory of Frank White, a local resident. As the elders tell the story, an argument broke out between some youths and a driver who forced his way into the street block party, pointing a gun at the children. That's when Frank White stepped in to protect them and the gunman shot him on the spot.

Today the garden is run by the nonprofit Brotherhood/Sister Sol, who has made the garden into an environmental learning center, and grows many varieties of fruits and vegetables. Frank White would be so proud.

Left: Mural painted on sheetrock boards; Right: Garden plot decorated with bricks and children's hand-prints
Following page: Colorful tires and fish pond

10

FRIENDSHIP GARDEN (WICKED)

In 2007, off upper Broadway near the Dance Theatre of Harlem, this cool greenery got a big, artful boost from the Broadway smash hit *Wicked* and the production's Green for Good campaign.

The show, based on a novel by Gregory Maguire, is a political, social, and ethical commentary on the nature of good and evil, a very apropos setting for a community garden.

One of the show's scenic designers, Edward Pierce, put his talents to the garden, creating a Wizard of Oz-themed wonderland with a yellow brick path, an emerald piano and fantastical lampposts. Under the backing of the New York Restoration Project, and Bette Midler, the garden is now a small, but vibrant place run, by a dedicated group of volunteers.

WEBSITE:
https://www.nyrp.org/green-spaces/
garden-details/friendship-garden-
wicked

ADDRESS
499 W. 150th Street between
Broadway & Amsterdam Avenue

HOURS
April to October 31st
or when the gate is open

Theme from the Land of Oz, painted by set designers of the Broadway musical "Wicked"

Walking around the tiny paths one feels an immediate admiration for the community's efforts to turn this once empty lot into a place of enchantment and grace.

Art exhibits, movie nights under the stars, birthday parties, and barbecues take place here, and of course a Halloween celebration, where witches and goblins freely roam about, beguiling young and old alike.

Add vibrant flowers, such as roses, lilies, hostas, hydrangeas, and you have not only good vibes, you've got good witches and friends.

Left: 1. Installation by artist Andrea Arroyo 2. Nick and his dog 3. Themed paintings inspired by the Land of Oz
Right: Tool shed with gigantic clock and stars

11

CONVENT GARDEN

Julia "Miami" Davis, a transplant from Florida, sits on her favorite bench and opens a can of tuna, her lunch for the day. In her mid-seventies, Julia is slim and vibrant with an opinion about everything. When she speaks she requires undivided attention. This is *her* garden and she is the queen.

"You can't take a photograph of me as I'm eating," she coquettishly smiles.

I compliment her on how great she looks and she waves me away with her hand. "Thirty years ago I was diagnosed with a heart condition. The doctor told me that if I didn't have surgery I'd be dead in three months. I walked out of his office never to return, and look at me still alive and well now. God and this garden have given me everything."

Gazebo under cloudy sky

WEBSITE:
Unavailable

ADDRESS
W. 151st St. Nicholas &
Convent Avenues

HOURS
April to October 31st
or when the gate is open

Convent Garden, smack in the heart of Sugar Hill, stands on the site of a former gas station that was demolished in 1985. Activist Luana Robinson tried to convert the space into a park, but her petition was blocked when underground gas tanks were uncovered. The site fell into total disrepair until Julia stepped in, cleaning up the plot with the help of community volunteers. The city noticing her effort, gave her a modest grant, which she used to purchase sod. Julia continued to add new features, creating a cobblestone path and planting trees and hundreds of flowers.

Left: Chairs for sale; Right: Creative corners by street found objects

Today Julia, surrounded by her grandchildren, is a keen observer of the neighborhood and this blooming gathering place for news and gossip that she controls. The garden is named after the Convent of the Sacred Heart, which was located nearby and burned down in the late 19th-century.

"You must come by at Christmas when I light up the entire garden. It's really something not to be missed," she says, spreading her arms to take in and invite me to all of it.

Left: Julia's imagination at play; Right: "Harlem Pietà"

12

HOPE: THE FRIENDLY GARDEN ON THE HILL

Winding paths, twisting and turning among lush foliage. A small gazebo with metallic chairs giving the impression of another time. A vegetable garden overgrown with ripe tomatoes. A large evergreen with a gigantic bow wrapped around it.

Hope on the Hill is built on top of the old Croton aqueduct that brought water to Manhattan via the High Bridge, flowing through underground channels beneath St. Nicholas and Amsterdam Avenues on its way to the reservoirs of Central Park and Bryant Park.

Because of the availability of water, flowers bloom everywhere here, interspersed with wild greenery, adding a mysterious feel to the garden. The space is so big, meandering between two city blocks, it takes me a while to notice the many volunteers quietly tending their plots and corners.

WEBSITE:
https://www.facebook.com/
Hope-the-Friendly-Garden-on-the-
Hill-915002278610088/

ADDRESS
459 W. 152nd Street between
Amsterdam & St. Nicholas Avenues

HOURS
April to October 31st
or when the gate is open

Red steps of old neighborhood building

Everyone is welcoming, eager to speak about the garden's history and point things out.

"You see those red steps? They're remnants of the adjacent building," a long-time volunteer explains. "It burned down in the '70s, but the steps were left intact, so we decided to keep them."

Others introduce me to their individual plots and their hard labor of putting up stone borders to stop water seepage or the seed incubators warming the soil so that the plants will be at a good start.

Left: 1. Discarded Coca Cola garbage cans used for compost 2-3. Ripe tomatoes and flowers 4. Sculpture, artist unknown
Right: Grape vine trellis

Nothing is left to chance. Winters can be brutal and the garden is often faced with multiple problems such as erosion and torn trees.

A hammock swaying under an enormous willow tree draws me closer. I'm about to try it out when I realize that a cat with stunning silver fur has already made herself comfortable on it. She peers at me with half-closed eyes but does not move. This is my garden, she seems to be telling me. I bow to her wishes and walk away.

Left: Ripe tomatoes; Right: Plants growing in seed incubators; Following page: Christmas ribbon and tomato plots

13

WILLIAM A. HARRIS GARDEN

Lori greets me with a wide smile. "Welcome! Come join us."
I walk up the steps that lead to the garden, the only garden
in Harlem raised above street level. A group of people is gathered
below a trellis, among them Lori's niece and brother-in-law.
Their kindness and hospitality are infectious.

Lori walks me around, pointing out with pride the flowers and
plants. A beautiful mural decorates the north wall, depicting a man
flanked by two young women. "This is my father, William Harris,
the one who started this garden," she tells me, "and the young
women are my sister and me."

A native of Virginia, William Harris relocated to New York after
serving in the Army in World War II. He then worked in the city's
sanitation department for thirty years.

WEBSITE:
https://www.facebook.com/
Hope-the-Friendly-Garden-on-the-
Hill-915002278610088/

ADDRESS
W. 153rd Street between
Amsterdam & St. Nicholas Avenues

HOURS
April to October 31st
or when the gate is open

Blooming coneflowers

After his retirement, and with the help of the local kids, he cleaned up and tended this undeveloped lot. As the years passed, Harris planted more and more, and the small corner soon turned into this thriving community garden overflowing with vegetables and flowers.

I looked at Lori and then at the mural. Two generations captured on this wall and I'm privy to know about it. I ask to take her photograph in front of the mural. She brings over her niece and brother-in-law. The story is now complete.

Left: Lori Harris with her niece and cousin under mural depicting her father, sister, and herself at a young age; Right: 1. Stone barbecue 2. Copper windmill 3. Wind chimes 4. Angel statue

14

MORRIS-JUMEL COMMUNITY GARDEN

It's early spring and there's still a chill in the air. A young man quietly works on his plot, while further away a woman is repairing a table. The first tulips have started to bloom, adding colorful touches to what seems to be a still dormant garden. Masks, mirrors, golden lion heads, and stone statues peer out from every corner.

This green gift is situated in the Morris-Jumel Mansion historic district and was part of the vegetable garden of an eighteenth-century estate.

The estate was built in 1765 as a summer house by Colonel Roger Morris for his wife, Mary Philipse and their family. The estate occupied approximately 135 acres of land that stretched from the Harlem to the Hudson rivers.

WEBSITE:
https://morrisjumelcommunitygarden.
wordpress.com/

ADDRESS
457 W. 162nd Street between
Amsterdam & St. Nicholas Avenues

HOURS
April to October 31st
Sat – Sun: Noon – 5 p.m.
Tue: 6 p.m. – 9 p.m. (Jun – Sept)

Hummingbirds on tin wall

With the outbreak of the American Revolutionary War, the Morris family abandoned their estate. In the autumn of 1776, General George Washington and his patriot officers moved in and made the house their headquarters. The superb views from Mount Morris made the location ideal for observing troop movements and General Washington used this advantage to plan his army's first successful victory; the Battle of Harlem Heights. In the end, peace won out. The garden rules.

Left: Plastic comedy and tragedy masks; Right: The garden in early spring

GARDEN INDEX

The decision of which of the so many existing gardens in Manhattan to feature was not an easy one. Because of space limitations, I could present only a few. Below is a full list of all gardens in the city, each one more enchanting than the other.

103rd Street Community Garden
105 E. 103rd Street

11 BC Serenity Garden
626 E. 11th Street

117th Street Community Garden
172 E. 117th Street

11th Street Community Garden
422 E. 11th Street

133rd Swing Street Garden
155 W. 133rd Street

6BC Botanical Garden
624-628 E. 6th Street

6th Street & Avenue B Garden
78-92 Avenue B

9th Street Community Garden & Park
703 E. 9th Street

Albert's Garden
16-18 E. 2nd Street

All People's Garden, Inc.
293-295 E. 3rd Street

Bradhurst Gardens Association (Garden of Love)
321 W. 152nd Street

Brisas Del Caribe
237 E. 3rd Street

Campos Community Garden
640-644 E. 12th Street

Carmen Pabon Del Amanecer Jardin
117 Avenue C

Carolina Garden (formerly 116th Street Block Assoc.)
102 E. 122nd Street

Carrie McCracken TRUCE Garden
145 St. Nicholas Avenue

Carver Community Garden
236-242 E. 124th Street

Children's Garden
194 Avenue B

Children's Magical Garden
131 Stanton Street

Clayton Williams Garden
303 W. 126th Street

Clinton Community Garden
436 W. 48th Street

Clinton Community Garden (LES)
171 Stanton Street

Columbia Secondary School Community Garden
1195 Amsterdam Ave

Corozal Family
170 E. 117th Street

Creative Little Garden
530 E. 6th Street

De Colores Community Yard & Cultural Center
313 E. 8th Street

Diamante Garden / Dimantis Garden
307 E. 118th Street

Dias Y Flores
520-522 E. 13th Street

Dorothy K. McGowan Memorial Garden
513 W. 158th Street

GARDEN INDEX

Dorothy Strelsin Memorial
Garden (Suffolk St. —
Committee of Poor People)
174 Suffolk Street

Earth People
333-335 E. 8th Street

East Harlem
Community Garden
429-433 E. 117th Street

East Side Outside
Community Garden
415 E. 11th Street

Edgecomb Avenue Garden
Park Sanctuary
339 Edgecomb Avenue

Edward P. Bowman Park
52 W. 129th Street

El Barrio Community Garden
415-421 E. 117th Street

El Cataño Garden
171 E. 110th Street

El Gallo Community Garden
1891-1895 Lexington Avenue

El Jardin del Paraiso
710 E. 5th Street

El Sol Brillante Garden
522-528 E. 12th Street

El Sol Brillante Jr.
537 E. 12th Street

Electric Ladybug Garden
237 W. 111th Street

Elizabeth Langley
Memorial Garden
121-123 W. 137th Street

Family Community
Garden Manhattan
156 E. 111th Street

Family Garden by
Tiffany & Co.
431 E. 114th Street

Fifth Street Slope Garden
626-27 E. 5th Street

Fireman's Memorial Garden
360 E. 8th Street

First Street Garden
48 E. 1st Street

Fishbridge Park Garden
338-340 Pearl Street

Five Star Gardens
252 W. 121st Street

Flower Door Garden
135 Avenue C

Frank White Memorial Garden
506 W. 143rd Street

Frederick Douglass Boulevard
Community Garden
301 W. 152nd Street

Friendship Garden (Lucille
McClarey Garden)
499 W. 150th Street

Garden of Love
302 W. 116th Street

Generation X Cultural
Garden
270-272 E. 4th Street

Green Oasis Community
Garden / Gilbert's Garden
372 E. 8th Street

Harlem Grown 131st Street
Farm
34 W. 131st Street

Harlem Grown 134th Street
Farm
116 W. 134th Street

Harlem Grown 134th Street
Green House
126 W. 134th Street

Harlem Grown P.S. 125
Community Garden
425 W. 123rd Street

Harlem Rose Garden
8 E. 129th Street

Harlem Valley Garden
197 W. 134th Street

Harlem Village Green
54 W. 129th Street

GARDEN INDEX

Oasis Community Garden
505 W. 52nd Street

Orchard Alley
350-54 E. 4th Street

Our Little Green Acre
(Garden Eight)
277 W. 122nd Street

Our Neighborhood Place
Abyssinian Development
77 W. 127th Street

P.S. 76 – Garden of
Perserverance
203 W. 120th Street

Pa'lante Community Garden
(110th Street Block Assoc.)
1651 Madison Avenue

Papo's Garden
220 E. 119th Street

Parque De Tranquilidad
314-318 E. 4th Street

Peaceful Valley
52 E. 117th Street

Peach Tree Garden
236-238 E. 2nd Street

Pleasant Village
Community Garden
342-353 Pleasant Avenue

Pueblo Unido
1659 Madison Avenue

RING – Riverside Inwood
Neighborhood Garden
236 Dyckman Street

Rev. Linnette C. Williamson
Memorial Park
65-67 W. 128th Street

Riverside Valley Community
Garden
699 W. 138th Street

Robert L. Clinkscales
Playground and
Community Garden
234 W. 146th Street

Rodale Pleasant Park
Community Garden
437 E. 114th

Sage Garden
281 E. 4th Street

Sam & Sadie Koenig Garden
237 E. 7th Street

Secret Garden
293 E. 4th Street

Serenity Gardens
522 W. 146th Street

Siempre Verde Garden
181 Stanton Street – 137
Attorney Street

St. Luke's Community Garden
435 W. 141st Street

Sugar Hill Park
333 Edgecombe Avenue

Toyota Childrens Learning
Garden (Coradan Evaeden)
603 E. 11th Street

Unity Park
55 W. 128th Street

Vamos A Sembrar
198 Avenue B

Walter Miller III Memorial
Garden (La Casa Frela)
13 W. 119th Street

West 104th Street Garden
8 W. 104th Street

West 111th Street
People's Garden
1039 Amsterdam Avenue

West 124th Street
Community Garden
75 W. 124th Street

West 132nd Street Garden
108-114 W. 132nd Street

West 181st Street
Beautification Project
814 W. 181st Street

West 87th Street Park
& Garden
55-57 W. 87th Street

William A. Harris Garden
W. 153rd St.

William B. Washington
Memorial Garden
325 W. 126th Street

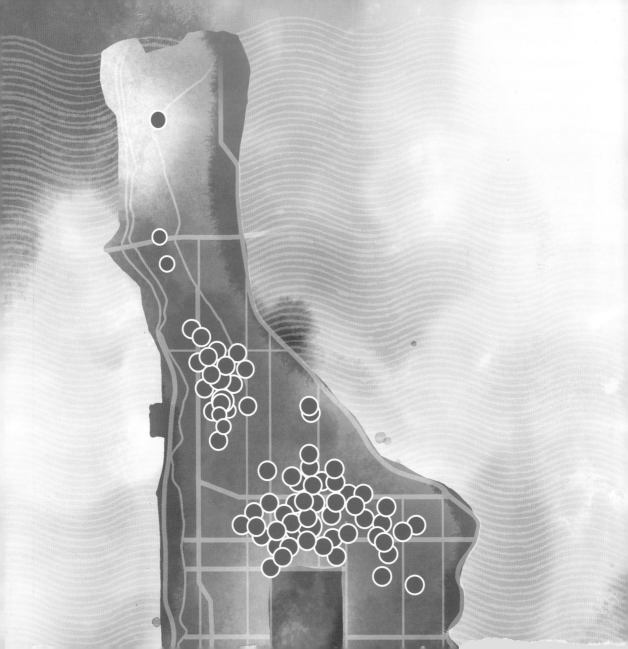

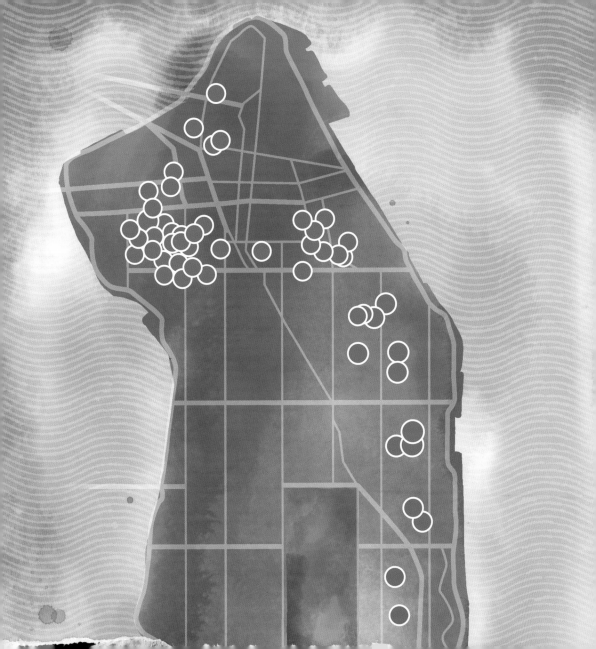

SPRINKLERS
THROUGHOUT
BUILDING

718-533-6800

ACKNOWLEDGMENT

Like the gardens themselves, *Rooted in the Hood* is the result of a group of people coming together and combining their visions and talents.

Among the many, I'd like to thank Gordon Goff for believing in this project and giving me the opportunity to share it; Kirby Anderson for her attention to detail; Roseanne Wells for helping me write an exquisite proposal; and Titika Angelidakis for reading the first draft and seeing its charms.

I also want to thank Bob and Betsy Goldberg for their generous sponsorship; TJ Gemignani for creating magic with his retouching work and for standing by me throughout this process; Donald Murphy for his enchanting watercolor maps; Cullen Thomas for his edits; and Walter Meyer for the book's title.

I also want to thank all of the people I've met in my wanderings and those who welcomed me into the gardens and shared their stories, including Maria Soares with her almost mystical knowledge of plants and flowers; Anne Boster for her gentleness and love of the earth; Jane Weissman for helping me identify the murals in La Plaza Cultural garden; Rolando Politi for his *Winter Flowers* sculpture; Lori Harris of the William A. Harris garden for posing under her family's mural; Miriam of the Humacao Garden for offering me apples and sharing the garden's history; and Marko Mavris for sharing his demolition stories in East Harlem during the '80's.

Finally, I'd like to sincerely thank this beautiful earth and all of its bounty.

Metal sculptures on Bowery

"I do not understand how anyone can live without one small place of enchantment to turn to." Marjorie Kinnan Rawlings

— For my family —